DR. SPOCK'S BABY BASICS

This concise and ready guide will help you
better understand your growing child
and provides invaluable practical advice on
day-to-day infant and toddler care.
You'll learn about:

Making a baby feel loved and secure

Providing good nutrition

Encouraging good sleep habits

Weaning a baby from a pacifier

Putting safety first when bathing a baby

and much more!

DR. SPOCK'S
BABY BASICS

BY ROBERT NEEDLMAN, M.D.

POCKET BOOKS

New York   London   Toronto   Sydney   Singapore

The ideas, procedures, and suggestions in this book are intended to supplement, not replace, the medical advice of your own physician. All matters regarding your child's health require medical supervision. Consult your physician before adopting the medical suggestions in this book as well as about any condition that may require diagnosis or medical attention.

The authors and publisher disclaim any liability arising directly or indirectly from use of this book.

An *Original* Publication of POCKET BOOKS

POCKET BOOKS, a division of Simon & Schuster, Inc.
1230 Avenue of the Americas, New York, NY 10020

ISBN: 978-1-4391-6941-4
ISBN: 1-4391-6941-1

First Pocket Books printing January 2003

10 9 8 7 6 5 4 3 2 1

POCKET and colophon are registered trademarks of
Simon & Schuster, Inc.

For information regarding special discounts for bulk purchases,
please contact Simon & Schuster Special Sales at 1-800-456-6798 or
business@simonandschuster.com

Printed in the U.S.A.

ACKNOWLEDGMENTS

A book like this one grows out of many years of experience, and so there are many people to thank. Thanks to Barry Zuckerman, M.D., now professor and chairman of Pediatrics at Boston Medical Center, for convincing me to train in developmental and behavioral pediatrics, and then supporting my growth and learning with unmatched mentorship. Thanks, too, to Steven Parker, M.D.; Margot Kaplan-Sanoff, Ed.D.; Deborah Frank, M.D.; John Kennell, M.D.; Karen Olness, M.D; and many other colleagues at Boston University and Case Western Reserve University. You have all taught me so much.

This book would not have existed without the vision, expertise, and hard work of many at The Dr. Spock Company, and, in particular, David Markus, who had the original idea, and Mona Behan, whose skillful editing and keen insights have contributed both polish and depth. The book is stronger for the meticulous, knowledgeable input of Lynn Cates, M.D. I'd also like to thank Mary Morgan for bringing the spirit of her husband of many years, Dr. Benjamin Spock, to us every day.

Thanks to my mother, Gloria Needlman, an early childhood educator who continues to teach me about children and parents; to my wife, Carol Farver, M.D., a pillar of support and steady common sense; and to our daughter, Grace, whose growing up has been an inexpressible blessing, and quite a lesson as well.

CONTENTS

INTRODUCTION

I am a baby watcher. Put me in a crowded place like a restaurant or an airport, and I instantly find the infant who is just discovering the world beyond his mother's arms, or the toddler who is scaling the seats like a climber challenging Everest. I watch how babies and their parents work together, sometimes smoothly, sometimes with friction. I'm always very curious, and I often find a way to start up a conversation. Talking with parents about their babies is what I do best.

As a pediatrician, I try to listen more than I talk. When parents come to me with concerns, they usually have a good idea of what they need. My first job is to convince them that I am willing—eager, really—to listen. After that, we work together to make sense of the situation. I don't believe in telling parents what to do. If I can shed new light on an old problem, parents usually don't have much trouble finding a solution that works for them.

This attitude is reflected in this book, as I've tried to write it the way I talk with patients: directly, in plain language, but without skimping on the content. The subject matter I tackle is simple, basic stuff—sleeping, feeding, comforting, and hygiene—but in my years of practice, I have been struck by how often it's everyday child-care issues, not major medical problems, that concern the parents of my young patients. A mom worries that she isn't providing adequate breast milk for her baby, a bleary-eyed dad wonders why his five-week-old infant isn't sleeping through the night yet, a couple wrestles with the thorny cloth-versus-disposable diaper debate. *Baby Basics* is designed to address some of these common and essential concerns, to give parents the information and confidence they need to tend to—and enjoy!—their infants and toddlers.

I've tried to provide plenty of practical advice as well as insights into babies' development—their abilities at different ages and the challenges they face—so that, as a parent, you can make informed decisions about what's best for you and your family. I've also tried to point out how everyday tasks such as feeding, bathing, and putting your baby to sleep are opportunities for emotional and intellectual growth. Not that every single minute needs to be packed full of meaningful learning—that would be too much pressure for any parent or baby—but I've tried to give you the facts you need so that you can reflect, from time to time, on the truly amazing journey you and your baby are taking.

The information in this book comes from several sources. I trained in general pediatrics at Boston City Hospital in the 1980s, and then underwent an additional three-year fellowship in developmental-behavioral pediatrics. This field sprang from the work of enlightened pediatricians such as Benjamin Spock, who was one of the first doctors in the United States to combine knowledge about children's physical health with insights into their mental and emotional development. Dr. Spock understood that parents care about their *whole* children, their heads and hearts, not just their muscles and bones. The words in this book weren't written by Dr. Spock, but the whole approach to thinking about children and their parents was inspired by him.

In fact, Benjamin Spock's timeless philosophy is the bedrock of The Dr. Spock Company, which was founded by a new team of pediatricians, obstetricians, and other experts to bring today's moms and dads the latest parenting and child-health information and advice. I have been vice president of developmental and behavioral pediatrics at the company since 2000, and my experiences have brought me a new kind of interaction with parents. As a staff writer for the company's website, drSpock.com, I've been able to contribute articles on a wide array of topics—everything from how to choose a preschool to how to explain the events of September 11 to children. I've also had the opportunity to answer parents' questions as part of our "Ask Our Experts" Q&A forum, and participate in *Parent Sense*, a series for public television that The Dr. Spock Company co-produced. Knowing that I was reaching a much larger number of families than I ever could have in any medical practice was both humbling and energizing.

While I was reading about the great ideas in child development and getting hands-on training from some of the very best developmental-behavioral pediatricians anywhere, I had another, equally influential teacher: my daughter, Grace. Grace taught me about the simple satisfaction that comes from bathing a baby, the fun of introducing a child to new and different foods, and the joy of taking long walks with an infant riding high in a backpack. My daughter also taught me a lot about sleepless nights and the many ways to calm a crying baby—or at least try to. Grace is now 13, and I'm still learning from her.

Still, perhaps my best teachers have been the hundreds of children and parents whom I've had the privilege to take care of over the years. Some have needed intensive treatment for serious medical, developmental, and behavioral problems. Many have needed only a little guidance or encouragement. All have taught me about children, parents, and families in ways that no textbook or master clinician could. These experiences, more than any other, gave me the confidence to know that the information in this book can be helpful.

But a book is only a book. *Baby Basics* not meant to be a substitute for personal medical care. If you find yourself feeling frustrated, concerned, or upset about your child, please talk with your child's doctor or another trusted professional, and find help. Parenting problems can be terribly painful and exhausting. No parent should have to face such challenges alone.

How to use this book
The book is divided into four main chapters, each dealing with a broad area of baby and toddler development: sleeping, feeding, comforting, and hygiene. The afterword wraps up themes that have appeared through-

out the book, tying them to the idea of what I consider another baby basic: values.

Within each chapter, topics appear in more or less chronological order, with newborn and baby issues first, followed by the issues most relevant to toddlers. The baby blocks on the top of every right-hand page clue you in to the age groups covered in the material on that page and the adjacent left-hand page (i.e., "N" for newborns, "B" for babies age two to twelve months, and "T" for toddlers, one to three years old). Notice that you won't always find the same age groupings as you go from chapter to chapter. This is because significant developmental changes occur at certain ages depending on the topic. For example, predictable and different sleep issues concern newborns, two- to five-month-olds, six- to seven-month-olds, eight-to-twelve-month-olds, and toddlers. They need their own sections. But the same issues that apply to comforting newborns, in general, also apply to older infants, while toddlers have their own distinct set of concerns; therefore, the Comforting chapter only has two age groupings: "Newborn and Babies" and "Toddlers." Sprinkled through the chapters are quotations from Dr. Benjamin Spock's timeless classic *Baby and Child Care* and also from parents writing on the bulletin boards of drSpock.com, our company's website. You can read *Baby Basics* from cover to cover, or skip to the topics that seem most relevant to the ages or issues that you're facing now.

The book isn't meant to be a comprehensive "how to" manual. The original *Baby and Child Care* still offers the broadest coverage of every aspect of parenting.

Instead, I've chosen to look in more depth at a few top-ics that are truly basic to raising babies.

Finally, this book doesn't offer easy answers to tough problems. Instead, I try to lay out the key issues and options, and trust you to choose. As a doctor, I can look parents in the eye and ask, "Did what I just said make sense to you? Will it help?" As a writer, of course, I don't have that luxury. I can only hope that as you read this book, you'll find some new ways of looking at babies and toddlers, some useful practical advice, and plenty of support for the good parenting you are already doing.

DR. SPOCK'S
BABY BASICS

CHAPTER 1

Sleeping

*"Allowing your child to fall asleep
on his own is going to take time,
patience, and earplugs."*

—**Happymama,** AS POSTED ON DRSPOCK.COM

What is it about a sleeping baby that makes grown-ups feel warm and happy? Babies, after all, do a lot of wonderful things while they're awake: They gaze at us, snuggle into our arms, and nuzzle our necks. But sleep, somehow, is special. The sight of a peacefully sleeping baby is powerful. It carries a message that all parents want to hear: Everything is all right; my small piece of the world is good.

For new parents, of course, a baby's sleep habits also have practical significance. Pregnancy is tiring, childbirth is exhausting, and taking care of a baby requires a great deal of energy. New parents desperately need sleep, but time to sleep is often in short supply. A baby who lets his parents get a good long rest, especially at night, is a real blessing. A baby who perks up when the sun goes down can feel like a tiny tormentor.

Sleeping

If you're lucky enough to have a so-called "good" sleeper, you may not have to think much about your baby's sleep habits. Of course, you'll need to follow basic safety rules—for example, choosing appropriate bedding and putting your baby to sleep on his back for the first six months of life. It also will help to have a predictable, relaxing bedtime routine. But beyond that, your baby's sleep habits may take care of themselves. On the other hand, there's a very good chance that things won't be that easy. Believe it or not, babies aren't born knowing how to sleep—it's a learned skill, and one that your baby will probably need your help to master. And even when he's well past infancy, your child may develop a few kinks in his nighttime routine.

This chapter will help you better understand your child's sleep habits and deal with many common problems and issues. Maybe your baby sleeps seven hours straight one night, then wakes up four times during the next evening. Maybe you're not certain whether to comfort, feed, diaper, or simply ignore your infant when he cries in the middle of the night. Maybe you need help deciding whether to put your child down in his own crib in his own room or let him share your bed. And then there's the whole thorny matter of dealing with bedtime resistance at different ages. This chapter contains all the essential information you need—everything from the proper infant sleep positions to handling an imaginative toddler's fear of monsters under the bed—so you and your child can both rest a little easier, a little sooner.

Sleep Basics

Sleep is important (even if we're not sure why). Despite decades of careful study, scientists don't completely understand the true purpose of sleep. Some believe that it's when we turn short-term memories into long-term ones. Sleep also seems to enhance our immune systems; that may be why we feel like sleeping a lot when we get sick and why we're more vulnerable to colds, sore throats, and other common infections when we're overtired. In babies, sleep might contribute to brain development, helping to maintain and organize all the wonderful new skills and information they pick up every day. Research also has shown that children do most of their growing while asleep—another good reason to ensure that your baby gets all the rest she needs.

Babies' sleep needs vary

Although all-too-brief naps and frequent night wakings may fool you into thinking your baby isn't getting much sleep, in reality she is probably getting plenty. The average newborn sleeps on and off for more than 16 hours a day. Although the amount of time spent asleep gradually decreases over time, by 12 months of age, most babies still sleep anywhere from 12 to 16 hours a day. Typical two- and three-year-olds need 12 to 14 hours of sleep a day, counting both nighttime sleep and naps.

KEY: Ⓝ =Newborn (0-2 mos.) Ⓑ =Baby (2 mos.-1 yr.) Ⓣ =Toddler (1-3 yrs.)

Sleeping

Each baby develops an individual pattern. There are sleepy babies, and babies who sleep relatively little. For the most part, these differences are probably inborn. Parents who get by happily on little sleep often seem to have babies who also sleep less than average (genetics is a powerful force!). But over time, how parents behave toward their babies also influences how much their little ones sleep. On the whole, babies who are cared for in a way that is very calm and predictable spend more time asleep. In fact, they tend to be more laid-back in general—more willing to sit quietly and let the world come to them, less intense in their expressions both of sadness *and* of happiness.

BEAUTIFUL DREAMERS

Compared with older children and adults, babies spend about twice as much time asleep in dreams. During dreaming, the brain is very active electrically and takes up more protein, the basic building block of cells and tissues. This goes along with the idea that dreaming is a key part of the learning process, a time when certain experiences that a child has had during the day are locked into long-term memory. In fact, it may be that infants dream so much because they are learning so much during the few hours that they are awake.

CLASSIC SPOCK
*"How much should a baby sleep?
Parents often ask this question, but
the answer varies from child to child.
In general, as long as babies are satisfied
with their feedings, comfortable, get
plenty of fresh air, and sleep in a cool
place, you can leave it to them to take
the amount of sleep they need."*

— Dr. Benjamin Spock, *Baby and Child Care*

Sleep patterns change

While the total amount of sleep doesn't change that much over the first few years, the *pattern* of sleep does in two very important ways: First, babies switch to sleeping more at night and less during the day. Second, they bundle their sleep into longer and longer blocks. Just after birth, for instance, the longest block of sleep is usually only about four hours or so; by one year, most babies are sleeping 8 to 10 hours at a stretch. For parents, of course, this difference is huge! As far as naps are concerned, toward the end of the first year, most infants are down to two naps a day; between 12 and 18 months, they'll probably give up one of these. By age two to three, most give up napping altogether, or have just a short afternoon nap.

5

Sleep Issues at Different Ages

From learning to tell day from night to dealing with nightmares, young children often need a little help from their parents when it comes to sleeping. Here is some essential information about common problems and the developmental issues that might affect your child's sleep habits at different ages.

NEWBORNS

In the 1980s, when I started in pediatrics, doctors routinely told parents that babies should sleep face down. That way, the theory went, the babies would not choke if they happened to spit up while asleep. It turns out that this was simply wrong. Babies spit up, all right, but they are actually less likely to choke when lying *face up*. Even more important, babies who sleep on their backs are much less likely to die of Sudden Infant Death Syndrome (SIDS, also called crib death). SIDS is diagnosed when an infant one month or older dies suddenly with no apparent cause, usually in his sleep. SIDS is a problem of little babies. Once a child reaches six months of age, the risk goes down substantially.

The amazing thing about SIDS is that it is largely preventable. The scientific evidence is overwhelming. All around the world, the rate of SIDS dropped off sharply as parents learned to put their babies to sleep on their backs. Since the "Back to Sleep" campaign began in the United States in the 1990s, the number of SIDS deaths has been cut in half. That is a tremendous number of babies whose lives have been saved by this simple advice.

A few points to keep in mind:
• **Some babies with special medical conditions do need to sleep on their fronts or sides.** Your baby's doctor will tell you if this is the case. For almost all babies, though, "Back to Sleep" should be the rule.

• **Sleeping on the back is safer than on the side.** Babies put to sleep on their sides often end up face down, as they move about during the night.

• **A firm crib mattress is critical.** Soft, fluffy mattresses, fleeces, and waterbeds are not safe. They increase the risk of suffocation.

• **Don't put stuffed animals or pillows in bed with your baby.** They, too, can increase the suffocation risk.

• **Babies shouldn't be overly warm when they sleep.** A blanket sleeper (also called a sleep sack) or soft "onesie" may be all your child needs. If you use a blanket, tuck it in firmly under the edges of the mattress, so that it cannot ride up by mistake and cover your baby's face.

• **If your newborn sleeps in your bed, make sure that you observe the same safety standards as above:** baby on his back, firm bedding, no waterbeds, no fluffy or loose blankets or pillows. (See "The Family Bed" section on page 48.)

• **Protect your baby from secondhand cigarette smoke.** It's not enough to refrain from smoking in the baby's room, because smoke drifts all through the air in your home. It's safest to make the rule that nobody smokes inside. Period. And if you still smoke, it's best to put on a

---

THE COLIC-SLEEP CONNECTION 🐜

Most babies go through a stage of fussy crying. It starts around two or three weeks of age and peaks at about six weeks. In extreme cases, the crying can average more than three hours a day, a heart-wrenching and trying condition known as colic (see Chapter 3 for more about colic).

It's interesting that the crying usually peaks right around the time a baby starts to shift from daytime to nighttime sleep and typically ends around three months of age, just when most babies complete the day and night transition. I don't think this is a coincidence. If you've ever experienced jet lag, you know that it can be very uncomfortable to have to change your sleep schedule. It may be that the strain of having to shift sleeping schedules contributes to the normal fussy stage—and, in the extreme, to infant colic.

---

jacket while you smoke outside, then take it off before picking up your baby. Smoke clings to fabric.

Are there any drawbacks to "Back to Sleep"? Yes. Babies who spend a lot of time lying on their backs sometimes develop flat spots on their heads. These are not dangerous in any way, and a flat spot is *nothing* compared with SIDS! Also, there are things you can do to prevent flat spots: Give your baby plenty of time to play on his tummy while he is awake and you are watching him. (This tummy time also helps him develop the strength in his arms and back that he needs to crawl.) Also, get in the routine of switching your child's orientation in his crib every couple of days (in other words, alternating where you place his head and feet). Babies tend to turn their head to the side so that they can see into the room. Changing their position in this way keeps equal pressure on both sides of the head, reducing flat spots.

Newborns confuse day and night
If it seems that your newborn is sleepy during the day and turns into a live wire at night, you're right. Most babies are born with night and day reversed. Experts don't know exactly why this is so. Perhaps it has to do with the fact that babies in the uterus tend to be the most active when their mothers are resting, and quietest when their mothers are active. This day-night reversal usually begins to change around six weeks of age, and between three and four months, most babies flip their schedules, sleeping much more at night, and much less during the day.

Don't expect a newborn to sleep all night

Although I've heard parents swear that their healthy new baby slept all through the night right from the start, I have to admit that I'm always skeptical about such claims. Newborns just aren't equipped to sleep all night long—their immature digestive systems require them to eat every few hours and to soil their diapers frequently. No wonder they typically waken several times a night, crying to alert their parents to attend to their very real needs. If your newborn baby actually does sleep for six or more hours at a stretch, be sure to mention this to your pediatrician or family doctor, particularly if you are breastfeeding; there's a chance that so much sleeping is actually a sign of illness.

Good habits start early

How you handle your newborn's nighttime routine has a profound impact on her future sleep patterns, and you'll both benefit if you get into good habits right from the start. The best way that parents teach their babies the difference between day and night is to be exciting and playful during the day, and calm and low key—or even downright boring!—at night.

During the day, be sure to give your newborn lots of loving attention, affection, and stimulation, being sensitive to her moods and basic temperament. When she starts getting bored, you can put a little more cheerful energy into your voice or make your face more animated. You can tell when your baby starts to get overstimulated. She'll frown, look away, yawn, or hiccup. You might even notice that the skin around her mouth looks a bit pale—a sign that she is a little stressed. The best way to respond to these signals is to slow down, make your voice soft and soothing (or stop talking altogether), look away slightly, and, in general, give your baby a little breathing room. She might fall asleep, or she might be eager for more play after a brief respite. She'll let you know. By "listening" to your baby in this way and letting her take the lead, you help her stay awake and alert for longer and longer periods during the day. And that helps her to sleep more at night.

Nighttime calls for a completely different strategy. When you tend to your baby at night, it's best to do just what needs to be done, but not much more. If

---

NOISE AND NAPTIMES

Often, parents think that babies require total silence while they're napping. But it's actually good for a baby to get used to sleeping with a reasonable amount of routine household noise in the background. Go ahead and run the dishwasher, listen to some music played at moderate levels, chat with a friend over the phone—chances are, you won't be disturbing your baby at all. In fact, if your child gets used to sleeping in absolute silence, he'll soon lose his innate ability to sleep through a normal amount of household hustle and bustle.

---

your baby is wet, change her—quickly, quietly, keeping the light levels as low as possible. If she's hungry, feed her calmly without the usual conversation. If she's lonely or upset, pick her up for a few moments without much talk or playing, then gently put her back down to sleep. This can be easier said than done. It is hard to do just the bare minimum for a baby you love—especially if she's at her cutest in the middle of the night! But if you don't want to make nighttime into social time, you have to force yourself to be businesslike (but not harsh or mean, of course). Do what you need to do, and little more.

Amazingly, even very small babies learn from these experiences. They learn that when it's dark outside, Mommy and Daddy aren't very much fun; when it's light, things are more interesting and exciting. That makes them much more willing to give up your company during the wee hours once they are developmentally able to sleep through the night.

Don't be in a rush to fuss
Even though you want to respond to your baby's needs, it's important *not* to jump up and soothe your baby the minute you hear him stirring. All humans, babies included, wake up either partially or completely several times a night as they enter a certain phase of their sleep cycle. It's natural for babies to whimper, coo, or cry a little at these times, but if they're left alone, they'll usually settle themselves back to sleep. However, if Mom or Dad rushes in to rock, feed, sing, or cuddle them back to sleep, they don't have a chance to learn

this important skill—ensuring that their bleary-eyed parents will endure many more sleep-deprived nights. I'm not saying that you should ignore your newborn's crying altogether—remember, newborns do need attention a few times a night—but wait a few minutes before you go to your baby, just in case he manages to fall back to sleep on his own.

Start developing bedtime rituals at an early age

Bedtime rituals will take on increasing importance as your baby gets older, but you can start developing a comfortable routine right from the start. End your baby's day with peaceful, soothing activities. Just before bed isn't the time to play airplane or a boisterous game of patty-cake. Instead, give your baby a bath, hold him in your arms as you softly sing or read to him, rock him for a few minutes, then gently put him down. Try to stick to the same routine every night; it soon will be his signal that lights-out is just around the corner.

Many parents make the mistake of rocking or holding their babies until they are completely asleep. Some even drive their babies around in the car every evening! Once a baby is completely "out," the relieved parents tiptoe over to the crib and try to set down their little bundle of joy. But, 9 times out of 10, the moment a baby is out of the warm arms of his mother or father, he wakes up and begins to cry. So, the ritual starts all over again, except that the parent is even more tired out than before.

There is a simple way to avoid this trap. You need to put your baby to bed when he's drowsy but not fully asleep. While they may fuss at first, most babies quickly learn to feel comfortable lying in their cribs when they're drowsy and letting themselves drift off into sleep. Once your baby has mastered this skill—and it is harder for some babies than for others, to be sure— bedtimes become easier.

Sleeping and feeding are connected

Babies develop rhythms for sleeping and feeding, and these rhythms are connected to each other. After the first few days of life, babies develop a predictable cycle of activity: wake up, nurse or take a bottle, look around and socialize, fall asleep, repeat. As sleep begins to occur more and more at night, feedings switch more and more to the day. As I mentioned earlier, by about four months, most babies are physically able to go eight or more hours at night without eating.

The coordination of hunger and sleep is an example of how babies' behavior becomes organized over time. Early on, parents play a crucial role in supporting this organization, feeding their babies and putting them down to sleep on a regular schedule (although not an overly rigid one). In time, though, the babies take over the organizing for themselves, and, eventually, regular cycles of sleep and hunger become automatic.

Some babies are by their natures more regular in their rhythms than others. Regularity is an aspect of temperament, a baby's inborn behavioral style. If your baby is one who becomes hungry every four hours like clockwork, then it will be easy for you to plan your day around her feedings and sleep periods. But if your child has an underlying biological rhythm that is less regu-

Q: I've heard that bottle-fed babies sleep better than breastfed babies. Is this true, and why?

A: How a baby eats does affect how he sleeps. Both breastfed and bottle-fed babies learn to sleep through the night, but bottle-fed babies as a group sleep through the night sooner. The exact reason for this isn't known. It might have to do with the fact that breast milk is more readily digested than infant formula, and therefore tends to pass through the intestines in less time.
But if this seems like a great inconvenience for breastfeeding moms, remember that it's easy for a mother whose baby is asleep nearby to simply bring her baby close, offer a breast, and fall back asleep when the feeding is over. There is no standing up and fixing a bottle in a cold kitchen in the middle of the night!

lar—going now two hours between feedings, now five—it will be harder for you and your baby to get on the same schedule. As a result, she is bound to be hungry sometimes when you aren't ready to feed her, and may not be hungry at other times when you are ready.

You can help a baby to be more regular by setting up routines and sticking to them. But some babies have a very hard time fitting their biological rhythms into a schedule. This may be especially true of babies who are premature or who were sick a lot when they were new-borns. With these babies, it's important that parents be flexible enough to meet their needs. Otherwise, the babies are bound to be unhappy a lot of the time—either hungry or overstuffed, too sleepy to interact with their parents, or too active when the parents need to sleep.

Practical tips

• **Spend as much time as possible holding your baby.** Contact, especially skin-to-skin contact with your infant right up on your chest, has a calming effect that may improve his alertness, feeding, and sleeping. During the day, a cloth baby carrier gives your little one the warmth and security of being held while letting you have your hands free.

• **Nurse or offer a bottle when your baby is hungry.** While your ultimate goal is to get your baby on a reason-able schedule, at first it is even more important for him to be comfortable and develop good feeding skills. Remember, comfortable babies sleep better. Babies who fuss longer before getting fed can fall into a vicious cycle of irritability, poor feeding, and poor sleeping.

• **Get to know your baby's stress signals.** Every baby does things that let parents know when he has had too much excitement and needs a rest. These signals include yawning, turning away, jitteriness of the lower jaw, turn-ing pale around the mouth, spitting up, or closing his eyes. If you've been talking or playing with your baby and you see these signals, he probably needs sleep or simply a bit of quiet time. Premature and small babies, or those who have been ill, often can stand only a little bit of stimulation before they require some peace and quiet.

• **Wake your newborn after four hours or so.** Even though you'd think that more sleep is better, the goal is for your baby to have a regular sleep-eat pattern. New babies need to eat roughly every four hours, if not more often. A one- or two-week-old infant who sleeps six or eight hours at a stretch is too sleepy. After about four hours, try to wake up your baby and offer a feeding.

• **Be more interesting and playful during the day, and more businesslike and boring at night.** As I explain above, this is the best way to help babies sort out night from day.

• **Give your baby time to settle down on his own.** If you rush in the minute he starts fussing, he won't learn this important skill. If your newborn is sleeping in another room and you've installed a baby monitor, consider turning it down at night so that you don't hear every little gurgle and rustle coming from your baby's room; chances are, if he really needs you, he can cry loud enough to get your attention. (Infant monitors are sold as safety equipment, but careful research has failed to show that they actually make babies safer.)

• **Help your newborn find his own thumb.** Sucking a thumb or fist is one way little babies can calm themselves down. When they get older, such techniques allow them to sleep through the night. And, unlike a pacifier, a thumb never gets lost. Parents often view thumb-sucking as a negative habit, but it's really a natural and powerful way that babies soothe themselves, and most give it up naturally when they learn other self-comforting techniques as toddlers or preschoolers.

• **Get as much rest as you can, napping when your baby naps.** Even though the goal is for your baby to eventually stay awake more during the day and sleep more at night, in the beginning you will have to be awake a lot at night. If you are exhausted, you'll feel miserable and you won't be able to be as comforting to your baby as you'd like.

• **Don't be shy about asking for help from other family members, especially your spouse or partner.** Taking care of a new baby is hard work. Let others in the family assume some of your chores and responsibilities, such as cleaning or cooking, so that you can focus on your baby and keep up your own energy.

• And remember: **Always put your newborn to sleep on his back to reduce the risk of SIDS.**

TWO TO FIVE MONTHS

By four months or so, most babies are ready to learn to fall asleep on their own at a regular, predictable bedtime. Falling asleep alone, without having to be held and rocked, is a crucial skill because it will allow your child to sleep for a six- to eight-hour stretch at night without having to wake you up for help. It's also important because children who learn to fall asleep on their own around four months of age are much less likely to develop problems sleeping through the night when they are older.

Many parents believe that babies begin to sleep through the night at this age because it's when they begin eating solid foods. But while having a full tummy may help them drift off to sleep, the fact that most babies sleep through the night around four months probably has more to do with changes in their brains and their growing ability to soothe themselves back to sleep.

Brain development changes sleep patterns

As I mentioned in the newborn section, parents help teach their infants to tell night from day by being stimulating and playful during the daylight hours and low key and quiet in the evening. But there are other forces at work, too. Babies' brains are developing rapidly, which causes many changes in their behavior. Around four months, the brainwave patterns that are typical of newborns give way to more mature-looking brainwaves, like those of older babies and children. In effect, the brain of a four-month-old works very differently from the brain of a two-month-old! At the same time that the brainwaves during sleep are taking on a more mature pattern, babies begin combining several brief sleep periods each night into one or two longer ones.

An important change also takes place around four months in an infant's visual system, which affects her sleep. At birth and for the first few weeks, babies are quite nearsighted, able to see clearly only things that are about 9 to 12 inches away. (Wonderfully, this is just the distance they need to stare into their mothers' eyes when nursing.) Around four months, however, babies become capable of focusing on people and objects up to several feet away. They also can hold their heads up for longer stretches of time, especially if their bodies are supported in a lap or highchair. As a result, babies around four months become fascinated with the world around them. Now they have a strong motivation to stay awake for longer and longer periods during the day, just to look around! As their alert periods lengthen, so do their sleep periods.

Routines provide comfort

In order to understand the importance of bedtime routines to your baby, think about how you usually fall asleep at night. Chances are, you like to arrange the covers and pillow in a particular way, with your arms and legs positioned just so. If you share your bed with someone, you're sure to have designated which side of the bed you each sleep on—you always on the left, your partner on the right, for example—and you've probably fallen into a certain pattern of saying goodnight. If either of you changes the routine, it's harder to fall asleep. In fact, these patterns get embedded (so to speak!) into both your body and your brain, and it's hard to change them.

Now imagine a baby, five months old, who always falls asleep while cradled in her mother's arms. When she wakes up in the middle of the night—which all babies do—she will need to have her mother's arms around her before she is able to fall asleep again. And until those arms come, all the baby can do is scream. That's why young babies need to learn to fall asleep without having the parents right there. Instead, they can develop comfortable sleep routines of their own, such as sucking their thumb or cuddling up with a special blanket, allowing them to soothe themselves back to sleep.

Changes in sleep can be a sign of illness

Sometimes it seems as if a baby really cannot sleep at all. He seems comfortable in your arms, but soon after you lay him down he begins to fret or lets out a high-pitched cry as if he is in pain. He may fall asleep for an hour or two when he is completely exhausted, but wakes up uncomfortable and still tired.

Most parents become alarmed if they notice their baby behaving this way. And with good reason. In a young baby, these behaviors are signs that there may be something medically wrong. One possibility is an ear infection. Ear infections can be very uncomfortable, and the pain is often worse when lying down because pressure builds up in the middle ear. A condition called gastroesophageal reflux, in which stomach acid flows back up into the esophagus, also is aggravated when lying down. The acid causes painful heartburn, and even if the problem is treated with medication, the baby may remember the pain and become anxious and fretful when laid down.

More serious illness often causes babies to be sleepier than usual. They may wake, but remain drowsy, without their usual bright-eyed alertness. As a good rule of thumb, any sudden change in a baby's sleeping, either less or more, should be a red flag to consult with your baby's doctor, and probably have the baby examined.

Practical tips
• **Until she is at least six months old, *always put your baby down to sleep on her back.*** This precaution helps reduce the risk of SIDS, as I mentioned in the newborn section. (In fact, you'll notice that many of the newborn tips still apply to this age group.) When your baby's awake and you're there to watch her, be sure to give her plenty of opportunity to play on her tummy, to prevent the back of her skull from flattening from too much time on her back.

• **Put your baby down to sleep *while she is still drowsy*, before she has fallen completely asleep.** This is the single best thing you can do to help your baby learn the self-settling skills she'll need to sleep through the night, now and when she's older. Do this at night, and also before naps during the day.

• **When your baby makes noise in the middle of the night or even wakes up completely, don't rush in right away.** Instead, wait a bit to give her a chance to fall back to sleep on her own.

• **Help your baby find her own thumb to suck, if she hasn't already.** Thumb-sucking is a powerful way that babies this age calm themselves down when they are upset or bored. When they wake up in the middle of the night, they can use thumb-sucking to help get themselves back to sleep. Sucking stimulates reflexes that slow the heart rate and improve digestion, and generally puts babies into a calm state. Unlike pacifiers, thumbs never get lost. Some parents discourage thumb-sucking for fear that it will become a bad habit. But most babies give up sucking their thumbs once they become toddlers or preschoolers and learn other effective ways of calming themselves.

• **Start a simple and soothing bedtime routine.** Rock your baby, sing a lullaby, share a picture book, say a prayer, or recite a nursery rhyme. Over time, these routines become a powerful signal that helps active children learn to make the transition to sleep. Bedtime routines also are a great opportunity to spend some true quality time with your child, as she is sure to enjoy these comforting and companionable interludes with her parents.

• **Begin to move toward a regular, predictable bedtime and wake-up time.** Let your baby have some time awake in the crib alone to learn how to entertain herself. If she starts crying in earnest, however, you'll still need to step in promptly, so she understands that you are there to make sure she is all right and doesn't become overly upset.

SNORING AND SLEEP APNEA

If your baby starts making unusual sounds while he's sleeping—such as snoring, gasping, or grunting—it's best to let a doctor examine him. Sometimes the problem is nothing worse than a stuffy nose, but at other times, odd breathing sounds can signal serious illness.

Snoring may be a sign of obstructive sleep apnea, a condition that often runs in families or plagues very overweight children. Apnea means "not breathing." "Obstructive" is the explanation for why the child is not breathing: When the child is deeply asleep, the muscles that hold the airway open relax too much, and a part of the airway caves in, causing an obstruction. Snoring is the sound of air moving past this blocked area.

If the blockage is complete, no air goes past. Unable to breathe, the child wakes up gasping for air. Then, because he is so tired, he often falls right back to sleep. Since his airway blocks off every time he falls into a deep sleep, he never really sleeps well, and he wakes up tired.

If your child snores persistently, be sure to have him examined; if left untreated, obstructive sleep apnea can cause inattentiveness, negative moods, tantrums, school problems, and even serious heart problems later in life.

SIX TO SEVEN MONTHS

Six to seven months is usually a pleasant and exciting time in a baby's life. Most babies are sleeping six or eight hours at a stretch by now. If your baby isn't, this might be a good time to talk with his pediatrician or family doctor, or with a child-behavior specialist. The problem may simply be that your baby needs more time to mature and grow—as is the case with many infants who were born prematurely—or there may be another cause that can be discovered and resolved. For example, gastroesophageal reflux (or infant heartburn) can sometimes cause poor sleep. It can often be treated with special feeding techniques and medication. As discussed earlier, frequent waking also can be a habit that your baby has developed, and that you can help change.

Treat bedtime crying in a loving but firm manner
It's easy for a baby this age to fall into a certain pattern: You kiss her goodnight and leave the room. She wails. You reappear, cuddle and kiss her, say goodnight, and leave the room. She wails. And so on. Both you and the baby are trapped in a vicious cycle that in the end leaves everyone frustrated and overtired.

The standard advice is to "let your child cry it out." Once children learn that crying doesn't make their parents appear, they stop crying. A more positive way to think about this process is that you are allowing your child to learn the skills she needs to fall asleep on her own. Most babies who are healthy certainly can calm themselves down and drift off to sleep. But if parents always do the soothing for them, they never have a chance to develop these important abilities themselves.

Letting a baby cry at bedtime usually works, and it is almost certainly the fastest solution. But it is not for everybody. Many parents simply cannot bear the thought of walking out of the room while their baby is wailing. Some worry that it is physically or psychologically harmful to let a baby go on crying, especially if the crying lasts for 30 minutes or longer. I actually don't think this is true. There isn't any good reason to believe that crying at bedtime is dangerous or harmful if a baby is not hungry or wet and is well loved and responded to at other times. Still, if you feel terribly uncomfortable letting your baby cry, then you should listen to your heart. There is another, gentler way of teaching a child to self-calm at bedtime, which I describe below.

Ferberizing is a popular approach
The cry-it-out approach is sometimes called "Ferberizing," after Richard Ferber, author of the now classic book, *Solve Your Child's Sleep Problems*. Ferberizing is based on sound behavioral principles: By coming back into the room, parents reward their babies for crying, without (of course) meaning to. Once you stop rewarding a given behavior, the behavior goes away.

In the best cases, babies cry for 20 or 30 minutes the first night, 10 or 15 minutes the second night, and by the third night, there is usually little if any crying before sleep. But behavioral principles also predict another result from this approach: When you stop rewarding a behavior (such as the crying), it often gets worse for a day or two before it goes away! Parents who don't know this ahead of time are often worried when their baby cries more the second night than she did the first. It's not unusual for a baby to cry for 30 or even 45 minutes for a few nights before learning to handle bedtimes alone.

Sometimes, however, the crying lasts even longer. Often, without meaning to, parents actually teach their babies to cry for longer and longer periods. They do this by waiting until they can't bear the crying anymore—say, after 15 or 20 minutes—and then break down and rock their baby to sleep. The next night, they endure 20 to 30 minutes of crying before rocking their baby to sleep. By the third night, their baby has learned that crying for a very long time eventually results in getting picked up.

The moral of this story is, If you decide to let your baby cry it out, you should be prepared to let the crying go on as long as it needs to. You need to brace yourself for a few rough nights, even though it's likely that the process won't end up being so hard. It's also helpful to warn any neighbors within earshot, so they won't think there is terrible child abuse going on. Usually, neighbors are sympathetic and supportive if they know what you're trying to do.

Letting your child cry does not mean, however, that you can't go in from time to time to check on her. You need to do this to reassure yourself, as well as your baby! You may have to change a diaper or rearrange the bedclothes. But you need to resist the temptation to hold your baby until she calms down (at which point, she's likely to fall off to sleep). If you don't, you run the risk of teaching her to cry for longer and longer, with the expectation that eventually she'll "win."

A more gradual approach also works

If all of this sounds too much like a battle, rather than a loving parent-child relationship, you might want to consider a gentler, but more time-consuming, approach: It begins with you sitting by the crib, perhaps even touching your baby with one hand, but not talking, holding, making eye contact, singing, or rocking. Once your baby is used to this routine and settles down easily, you can move a few feet from the crib, again without talking or making eye contact. When he accepts this arrangement, you may be able to move outside the door, and then leave altogether. Whatever you do at bedtime, you also have to do at naptime and when your baby wakes during the night.

This more gradual approach means that you never have to sit in another room listening to your baby cry out for you and not respond to him. On the other hand, it also may mean many tired nights of sitting in your child's room, not sleeping much yourself. This is a tough problem, either way you tackle it. As you go through the process—quick or slow—you will want to remind yourself of the goal: the wonderful night when you lay your baby down, give him a kiss goodnight, and simply walk out of the room, as he contentedly drifts off to sleep on his own.

Parental concerns can affect a child's sleep

Sometimes a baby's troubles at bedtime are a reflection of issues that the parents are struggling with. When a child has been ill, for example, or if the pregnancy has had some difficulties, parents sometimes come to believe that their baby is very fragile and would be hurt by crying. In other cases, the crying has become a focus for tension or anger between the spouses or partners. For instance, one parent might feel that the other is not doing a good enough job, while the other parent might be feeling criticized. If you find yourself in this uneasy position, it's important to get help. Your pediatrician may be able to reassure you if you bring up your specific concerns about your child's health. A marriage counselor, member of the clergy, or other professional may help you and your spouse communicate more effectively and give each other the support you both need.

Practical tips

• **Add picture books to your bedtime routine.** Simple nursery rhymes are a good choice. Babies love the sound of their parents' voices, and they find the rhyme and rhythm soothing. You don't have to read for hours; five minutes is a long time for a six-month-old to stay interested in a book, and even shorter blocks of reading time, if repeated regularly, still help your baby begin a reading habit that will last his lifetime. You also can make up a bedtime story or a nonsense rhyme, or choose a picture book without many words and make up your own to go with the illustrations or photographs.

29

PARENT TO PARENT

"The first night, it was heart wrenching to listen to our baby cry, but my husband kept saying to wait 20 minutes. So we waited, and he didn't take that long to soothe himself right back to sleep. Now he cries sometimes, but quickly gets himself calmed down and goes to sleep. It is WONDERFUL!!!"

— **kndeapple,** AS POSTED ON DRSPOCK.COM

If your baby begins to love books and reading aloud now, he'll be more likely to be able to pay attention to a whole story when he is an active toddler.

• **Keep bedtimes as routine as possible.** Start at about the same time, perhaps after a bath and "tooth brushing" (many parents use a soft cloth on their babies' gums to get them used to tooth brushing before bed). Keep the same order of events—for example, story, lullaby, kiss goodnight.

• **Continue to put your baby down to sleep at bedtime and for naps while he is still awake.** Let him fall the rest of the way to sleep on his own. That way, when he wakes in the middle of the night, he will be able to get back to sleep without disturbing you.

• **Avoid giving a bottle immediately before it's time to go to sleep.** Instead, give the last bottle or breastfeeding before beginning the bedtime routine. Food right before bed doesn't actually help children to sleep longer.

• **Don't put a baby to sleep with a bottle of formula or breast milk.** Once he has teeth, this practice is a sure recipe for severe dental cavities (or caries). Children and adults make less saliva during sleep, so any milk or other sweet liquid sits on the teeth and isn't washed away. The bacteria that feed off those sugars produce acids that eat into babies' teeth, causing cavities.

EIGHT TO TWELVE MONTHS

Around eight months or so, many babies who were sleeping through the night start waking up again. This unwanted change is so predictable that I always mention it to parents when they bring their babies in for their six-month checkups. Then, when the night waking shows up in a month or two, the parents aren't taken by surprise (and they think that they have a really smart pediatrician!).

Out of sight doesn't mean out of mind
The best explanation I've found for this phase is that it stems from a child's growing thinking and memory

31

abilities. Around the same time that she starts calling out in the night for Mommy or Daddy, a baby shows that she knows that objects still exist even if they are temporarily out of sight. If you show your baby a toy car, for example, and then hide it under a cup, she goes right to the cup and lifts it up, fully expecting the toy to be there. Try this with a younger baby, say six months of age, and the baby loses all interest in the toy once she can't see it anymore. If she reaches for the cup, it's because the cup itself has caught her eye; she is surprised to find the toy under it.

How does this developmental stage connect with sleeping (or rather, *not* sleeping)? Once a baby remembers that Mom and Dad are in the next room even if they are temporarily out of sight, she is much more likely to call out for her parents, demanding that they return. If you are the tired parent stumbling into your nine-month-old's room in the middle of the night, it may comfort you to know that this behavior is really a sign that your baby is becoming smarter. Also, you might notice that your child develops a temporary disruption in her sleep habits when she makes a major developmental leap—learning to walk or put two words together, for example. It's as if the cost of these gains is difficulty falling or staying asleep.

Don't encourage nighttime feeding
Before I suggest a few things you can do to ease any sleep problems with children this age, I want to mention one mistake parents frequently make: feeding their babies when their little ones wake at night.

Although it may be tempting to offer a bottle or breast to calm a fussy baby, by six to eight months, most healthy babies don't need to eat in the middle of the night. However, they're only too happy to have a snack in the wee hours if you begin giving them one, and it can become a habit that's hard for them to break. Night feedings also are a bad idea because if children fall asleep with milk or juice clinging to their teeth, they are prone to get tooth decay. To prevent this, give only water in a bottle or cup during the night—no threat to their teeth and much less interesting than milk or juice, so they won't mind giving it up so much. And if you do offer your baby a bottle filled with water, don't leave it in the crib overnight. When babies drink a bottle lying on their back, fluid can run down into their ears, making them more prone to middle-ear infections.

Practical tips
• **Continue to put your baby down to sleep when she is still drowsy, not fully asleep.** Babies who can fall asleep on their own are more likely to be able to fall back asleep when they wake in the middle of the night.

• **When your baby wakes in the middle of the night, wait for a minute or two to give her a chance to fall back asleep independently.** Far from being hard hearted, you're helping her learn an important skill.

• **If you need to go into your baby's room to resettle her, try to be calm and even a little boring.** If your baby is fully awake, you may need to repeat a bit of the bed-time ritual before going back to your own room.

• **Stick to a predictable bedtime routine.** A regular routine is especially important now that your baby is more likely to express her own will and desires. Knowing that things happen in the same way every night gives young children a sense of security and control that is very calming. So give your baby a bath, settle down and look at a picture book together, tell her a story or sing her a song, give her a kiss, and tell her goodnight in the same way every evening—whatever affectionate, soothing routine you've worked out that helps her make the transition from day to night.

TODDLERS

As children enter the toddler years, new challenges arise. Falling asleep means saying goodbye to the exciting activities of the day, and especially, to parents. It means coping with being alone. Young toddlers may be so dazzled by the newfound thrill of walking that they work on mastering it almost non-stop, and fall off to sleep only when they are dead tired. They probably dream about walking! Older toddlers may start getting anxious at night, or wake frequently with nightmares.

Expect bumps on the road to independence
One reason bedtime is so hard for so many families is that children and parents alike have strong feelings

about independence and connection. Children have a natural, inborn need to feel connected to and protected by their parents. But starting around nine months or so, they also have powerful urges to explore and to be on their own. The pull and tug between these two needs—dependence and independence—is what fuels a lot of toddler tantrums. It's not only that toddlers want their own way. They want to be completely in control and free, and they also want to feel completely connected *at the same time*.

Parents have mixed feelings about independence, too. We want our children to know that they will always belong to us, but we also want them to stand on their own two feet, go off to daycare and then school without us—and go to sleep on their own. We expect our young children to handle these separations, but we often harbor secret doubts. We wonder, Will they really be all right? Children tend to be amazingly sensitive to their parents' emotions. If they detect that we are anxious, even though we try to reassure them or act confident and firm, they become even more uncomfortable with the separation. And as they become more and more upset, we become convinced that they really can't handle the situation.

For example, a parent may worry that his child will be scared to be left alone at bedtime. Then, at the child's first sign of distress, the parent becomes certain that he really is terrified. The child observes his parent's upset face, and now he really does become frightened! Of course, I am not suggesting that you should ignore a child who is truly scared. But parents need to allow their children to experience a little bit of anxiety, so that the children can learn to overcome it on their own—an extremely important life skill.

Separating from a child at bedtime can be especially hard for parents whose work keeps them away all day. If parents get home at 6:00 P.M. and bedtime is 7:30, there really is almost no time in the day for togetherness. Under the circumstances, it's completely understandable that a parent might not say goodnight with the loving but very firm tone that tells a child, "Now it's time for you to fall asleep, and I know that you can do it and that you'll be fine."

The reason I'm focusing on how parents sometimes play into bedtime problems is not to cast blame, but to help you take a fresh look at your own bedtime behavior, and perhaps choose to do things differently. For example, if you know that you tend to feel guilty about leaving your child alone in bed, you might ask yourself, Is my concern realistic? Am I giving my child a chance to develop his ability to soothe himself? If you feel as though bedtime comes too soon, you might consider making his bedtime later, as long as he can sleep later in the morning. Babies and young children need a lot of sleep, but it doesn't have to begin by a certain hour.

Be wise to their tricks—and tantrums!

Many toddlers try to delay the inevitable separation at bedtime by asking for multiple stories, cups of water, trips to the bathroom, and so on. These demands, while sometimes cute, can almost take on a desperate tone as a child tries to come up with yet one more task for his exhausted parents. To prevent endless bedtime delays and avoid the tantrums that your refusal might trigger, set limits ahead of time. "We're going to have two stories, one cup of water, one trip to the bathroom, two hugs and three kisses, then goodnight." The trick to making this preventive strategy work is consistency—picking a routine and sticking to it. If your child asks for more, explain that he can have only "two stories, one cup of water, one trip to the bathroom," etc. In other words, simply repeat yourself. If your child presses you to explain why, the best reply is "Because that's what we do at bedtime." Believe it or not, most toddlers (and even preschoolers) are perfectly satisfied by this sort of circular explanation.

Another effective tactic is a three-step approach: Acknowledge what your child wants, state the limits, and end on a hopeful tone. For example, you might say, "I know that you'd like more stories and you don't want it to be time for sleep. But it is time for sleep, and we have to stop the stories now. We'll have more stories in the morning."

Keep your cool

You may feel frustrated by your child's unending demands, but getting angry doesn't help at all. It only invites her to become upset, thus delaying bedtime (exactly what she wants). If you feel yourself becoming angry, it's best to say goodnight rather quickly and go to a part of your home as far from your child's room as possible. Make a cup of tea. Open a magazine. Ignore your child's pleas and cries—as long as you know that she is actually not in danger or pain—and calm yourself down. Chances are, by the time your nerves are settled, your child also will have settled down and fallen asleep.

If your child follows you out of the room, gently put her back in bed, remind her lovingly but firmly that it's time to go to sleep, and leave. You might have to repeat this several times for a few nights before your child learns the drill and stops getting out of bed. But if you're firm and matter of fact, she'll soon tire of this rather boring game.

Early risers can cause problems for sleepy parents

Some folks are naturally morning people and others are more wide-awake in the evenings. If your child is a morning person and you're not, you may have a problem on your hands. Sometimes the problem is due to something simple, such as too much light or noise in your toddler's room, which you probably can fix. Other times, the problem is that your child wakes up partway and can't settle himself back to sleep, even though he's still tired. This early-morning waking is basically the same as middle-of-the-night waking, which I discussed earlier.

Sometimes, though, a toddler really is wide-awake and raring to go at 5 A.M. He may have gone to bed at 7 P.M., and those 10 hours of solid sleep were all he needed. If a child is not tired, there is nothing you can do to make him sleep longer or conform to your sleep schedule. Instead, you need to help your child learn ways of amusing himself until you're ready to get out of bed. Here are some suggestions:

• **Put a few interesting toys or toddler-proof books in your child's crib after he's fallen asleep.** When he wakes, he can discover them and may stay interested for a while. Be careful that all toys in the crib are safe—no small parts that could become choking hazards, no straps or belts that could pose strangulation risks, and no large toys that could help your child climb over the crib rail.

• **Get him used to a little time alone.** Give your child time each day playing by himself in his crib or in a playpen, so he becomes used to amusing himself.

• **Set an alarm clock in your toddler's room to play music when it's time for you to wake up.** Explain to your child that he needs to play on his own until the music comes on.

• **Consider making your child's bedtime later.** Usually this is simply a matter of starting the bedtime routine a few minutes later each night, until you arrive at the desired schedule.

Fear of the dark is common
It's normal for young children to be afraid of the dark. Their imaginations are powerful and they're still learning to tell the difference between what is real and what is make-believe. Nighttime fears seem quite real to them.

Sometimes you can fight fire with fire, using products of your own imagination to counter products of their imagination. For example, young children think that parents are all-powerful. You can use this to help calm nighttime fears by telling your child that you have the power to keep all monsters out of your house. You might make this even more tangible to your child by using what I call "Monster Spray": Hold your hand in spray-can position with your index finger on the imaginary nozzle. Explain that you are holding a can of magic Monster Spray, which is guaranteed to keep all monsters away. "Spray" the room, making a hissing noise, and be careful to spray under the bed and in the closet (both notorious monster hiding places). Be quite serious while you do this. Your child will know that you are pretending, of course, but he won't care.

Monsters that aren't banished with this type of magical reassurance sometimes are signs that your child is upset about something real, not just a figment of his imagination. Because children don't easily put concepts into words, their worries may take the form of monsters. For example, one little boy is terribly angry with his baby brother, but he knows that it's wrong to be angry—he's supposed to *love* his brother. So the anger turns into a monster in his closet. A monster's upsetting, but at least it's a more acceptable target for negative feelings and something he can ask for his parents' help with. Reassurance that it's OK to be mad at baby brothers (although it is not OK to punch them) may be all that the child needs to feel better and send that monster packing, at least for the moment.

If a child is truly frightened at bedtime, it does no good to take a tough stance and demand that he stay in his room. That just makes him feel more alone and scared. So you need to be able to tell if your child is really afraid or is simply using "I'm scared" as a way of roping you back into the room. For real fright, you may need to stay in your child's room to reassure him for a while. If the fear persists despite your efforts, you should talk with your pediatrician or a child psychologist to help your child deal with his fears.

Nightmares start in the toddler years

Starting around three years of age, if not before, every child has scary dreams from time to time. Your natural inclination as a parent probably is to reassure your child that everything is fine and that she is really safe. And that's just the right thing to do. It's often not very helpful to say, or imply, that a child is being "a baby" for being scared of a nightmare. This just makes the child feel ashamed as well as scared. Also, saying "it's *only* a nightmare" might make it sound as though you don't think it's important that your child is scared. A better approach is to let her know that you understand that nightmares are truly frightening and unpleasant. But also you should explain that dreams aren't real and that you are there to make sure your child is safe.

You may need to stay with your child until she's ready to fall back to sleep. It might help to bring along a book or knitting to pass the time. Some parents take their children into their own bed, which is certainly reassuring. But this can backfire if your child makes sleeping in your bed a habit. I think it works as well for a parent to sit alongside a child's bed, offering reassurance in the child's own room.

41

CLASSIC SPOCK
"When your child awakens from a nightmare, you should comfort her by telling her that everything is all right, that she was having a dream, and that dreams aren't real. Then you can ask her to tell you about the nightmare, so you'll know what issues to deal with. Continue to reassure her that it was a dream, like make-believe, and that you won't let anything bad happen to her in real life."

— Dr. Benjamin Spock, *Baby and Child Care*

If nightmares are happening more than once or twice a month, along with reassurance, you'll need to reduce any exposure to scary or violent images or ideas that may be sparking the nightmares. I often prescribe a "no-violence diet," which means, among other things, protecting your child from television news, most cartoons, and scary stories. A very important part of the no-violence diet is for parents to take a hard look at how they are resolving conflicts or differences in their home. If they use angry words, shouting, threats, or physical force, it's very possible that these actions are raising their children's stress level and contributing to the nightmares.

Nightmares that occur often—more than a couple of times a week—and that aren't getting better with reassurance and the no-violence diet, may be a sign that there is significant stress in your child's life. Often, consultation with a pediatrician, child behavior specialist, or child psychologist can help you find and deal with the root of the nightmares.

Night terrors are terrifying for parents, too

It's 11:30 P.M. and your three-year-old sits up in bed with a terrified look on his face and glassy eyes. As you go to comfort him, he struggles and pushes you away. About 10 minutes later (it probably feels like a lot longer), he falls asleep. He wakes up in the morning and does not remember the event at all.

This is a classic night terror. Unlike nightmares, which are scary dreams, night terrors occur when a child is in a deeper stage of sleep. What looks like fear or agitation during a night terror does not come from scary images in the child's mind—in deep sleep, the mind doesn't make clear images, scary or otherwise—but from activity in other parts of the brain that have to do with fear. These are the parts of the brain that make the heart race, the palms sweat, and the eyes bug out. Children usually have no memories of their night terrors, although they sometimes remember waking up and finding their parents looking confused and upset.

Many young children who are completely healthy have night terrors from time to time. A child may have one a month, or as many as one or two a week. They may occur over weeks or months. Most children stop having them by age six or seven. Children under intense stress—for example, those who have lived through an earthquake—sometimes respond by having a lot of night terrors. But most of the children who have night terrors are experiencing only normal amounts of stress and are healthy in every way.

Night terrors aren't dangerous. Trying to calm a child down by holding him often only makes him more agitated. Trying to wake a child from a night terror is hard, because night terrors occur during a deep phase of sleep. If your child stays in bed and isn't moving around enough to hurt himself, it's probably best to simply let him be. If he tries to get up, you may have to hold him to keep him from bumping into furniture and hurting himself.

If your child's night terrors usually happen at about the same time of night—usually in the first few hours of sleep—try waking him up briefly before that time. Often, just interrupting the sleep cycle in this way is enough to prevent night terrors. In severe cases, medication can be useful, although most experts try other things first. Certainly, thinking about sources of stress in your child's life and doing what you can to ease some of the pressure is a good thing to do, and it might help with the night terrors, too.

Safeguard sleepwalking toddlers
Sleepwalking is like night terrors in that both occur when the child is in a deep, non-dreaming phase of

sleep. In both, the child is only vaguely aware of what's around her, and after she falls asleep again, she has no memory of the event. The main problem with sleep-walking is that children sometimes do things in their sleep that could be dangerous, such as walking out of the house and down the street. If you find your child sleepwalking, you can try all the same things that are suggested for night terrors. Also, it may be necessary to put a latch or gate on her bedroom door so that she can't leave her room and injure herself.

Resume bedtime routines quickly after an illness

When a child is sick, he feels uncomfortable and loses some of his ability to cope with the added stress of going to sleep. So it's natural for a toddler who had been handling bedtimes pretty well to start having more fear of the dark and needing more attention around bedtime when he's sick. Also, with some ill-nesses, such as ear infections, the pain may be worse when the child is lying down.

When your child is sick, it's also natural for you to relax the usual bedtime rules. You may decide to stay with your child until he falls asleep, or have your child sleep in your bed. In the short run, these changes make perfect sense. Be aware, though, that long-lasting sleep problems often begin after a child receives special treatment after a minor illness. The child gets used to being pampered and expects the rule-bending to con-tinue indefinitely. That's why it's a good idea to get back to the old routine as soon as you possibly can after a short-term illness.

Practical tips

• **Give your child plenty of active time during the day and in the evening, but not right before bed.** Instead,

---

IN PRAISE OF BLANKIES 🐾

Parents sometimes worry that having a blankie or other security object is babyish and try either to prevent their children from developing such a dependence or to take the object away from them at as early an age as possible. But this common habit really isn't babyish at all. Most babies don't create special objects for the purpose of giving themselves comfort. It's only by one and a half or two years of age that children are sophisticated enough to use this coping skill.

You also might worry that once your child's latched onto a special blankie or doll, she'll carry it around all day, like Linus in the Peanuts *cartoon. In fact, many children use their special objects only at night, and perhaps before naps. Others want to keep their blankies with them all the time. But around age five or six years, if not before, they become aware that few of their peers carry blankies, and they usually leave the beloved object on their beds. In fact, I've known very smart, successful teens who bring a special teddy bear along to college. It does them no harm!*

---

plan quiet activities such as reading aloud, reciting nursery rhymes, or singing.

• **Keep naps short.** Make sure that the afternoon nap doesn't last more than about an hour, and is over at least three or four hours before bedtime.

• **Stick closely to the bedtime routine you've established so that your toddler can anticipate what is going to happen.** For example, reading aloud might come first, followed by a special tucking-in ritual, and then a kiss just before you leave the room.

• **When your toddler wakes in the night, give her a few minutes to settle herself down.** If that fails, you'll need to check to see that everything is all right—that she doesn't need her diaper changed, for instance. Then use a shorter version of the bedtime routine, perhaps just the last two things, before leaving the room.

• **Help your child find a safe stuffed animal, blanket, or pillow to be her special bedtime companion.** Young children, with their powerful imaginations, are able to give magical calming powers to such objects. The "blankie" or "lovey" almost becomes a substitute for you, the parent. But, unlike you, the blankie stays with your child all night long, and for as long as she wants and needs it.

• **Keep crib critters small.** If your toddler is still sleeping in a crib, make sure that her stuffed animal or other lovey isn't large enough for her to climb on top of and thus get out of the crib. Picture books with cardboard or cloth pages are safe and interesting companions for the crib.

• **If your child is troubled by thoughts of monsters under the bed or other scary nighttime visitors, try offering magical reassurance.** For example, you might use "Monster Spray" or a "wizard's wand" to banish these nasty creatures. If your child has frequent nightmares, try putting her on a no-violence diet that eliminates her exposure to violent or frightening images on TV and in books or videos.

Sleep Options

Although people often have strong opinions on the matter, there is no single "right" way for children to sleep. People from different cultures sleep in different ways, just as they live differently during their waking hours. Different individuals also make choices about how to put their children to bed. What you choose will depend on your values and habits, as well as your child's temperament.

The family bed is the norm in many cultures
Many parents choose to share their bed with their baby, especially their newborn baby. In much of the world, this is the *only* way parents would ever consider putting a baby to bed.

Many here in the United States also have strong feelings about the matter, one way or the other. But apart from some important safety considerations, there is no clear-cut right or wrong. Here are a few of the pros and cons:

Pros:
• **Young children seem to like sleeping with their parents if they get a chance.** Even premature infants in their incubators have been observed to gradually move next to a warm, soft, rhythmically moving object, as though following a natural urge to sleep next to another body.

• **For breastfeeding mothers, having their infants in bed makes middle-of-the-night feedings much easier.**

• **The practice of children sleeping apart from other children and from their parents is quite new from the standpoint of human history.** In many parts of the world, co-sleeping is still very much the norm.

• **It is possible that co-sleeping promotes family togetherness, but there are certainly other ways to do that, too.**

Cons:
• **Having a child in bed means that parents have to find a different time and place for their sexual relations.**

• **Co-sleeping must be a free choice.** If a husband, say, only agrees because his wife insists, the family bed will probably result in resentment, not family harmony.

SIX SAFETY RULES FOR THE FAMILY BED

If you do choose to have your baby sleep with you in bed, it's especially important to follow these six basic safety rules for infant sleeping:

1. Babies should sleep on their backs, unless there is a medical reason for them not to.

2. They should sleep on a firm surface: no fleeces, feather beds, or waterbeds, etc.

3. Babies should be dressed lightly and comfortably, not over-bundled.

4. They should never be around secondhand smoke, whether awake or sleeping.

5. The American Academy of Pediatrics (AAP) advises that babies should not share a bed with adults who are not their parents or with other children; the children and other adults may not be as careful about following the safety rules.

6. The AAP also warns against sleeping on a couch with a baby, because of the risk that the baby will get caught between the parent and the back of the couch.

• If a child moves around a lot during sleep, it can be uncomfortable for parents, who find their sleep disturbed by little arms or legs poking them in the night. Also, children aren't the quietest sleepers in the world, and their whimpers, breathing, and babbling can make them less-than-welcome bedtime partners.

• Once started, co-sleeping may be hard to stop, at least for several years. So the decision is one that needs to be made with the long-term implications in mind.

Over-lying is a safety concern in some cases
Some doctors strongly advise against parents ever falling asleep with their baby in bed next to them. The main concern is that a parent might roll over on the baby and smother him. This is sometimes called over-lying. Most parents sleep very lightly if there is a baby in bed with them, and they wake up at the least hint of trouble. But there is a real danger of over-lying if :

• You are naturally a very sound sleeper, or are sometimes so overtired that you fall into a very deep sleep.

• You take medications or drugs that make you sleep especially soundly.

• You drink enough alcohol to make you sleep soundly and difficult to rouse.

If any of these things are true for you, then sleeping with your baby is probably too dangerous to try.

51

Sharing a bedroom, but not a bed, with your baby

You can have your baby in your room without necessarily having your baby in your bed, putting her in a cradle, bassinet, crib, or co-sleeper (see page 57). In fact, most American parents probably choose this option for their newborns and young infants for a number of good reasons:

• **New babies wake up frequently at night, for feeding, changing, or just to be cuddled.** If you have to get up and walk down the hall each time, you will get a lot of unwanted exercise.

• **It's understandable if you want to check on your new baby several times a night, "just to make sure she's all right."** New babies are not nearly as delicate as most parents think they are, but the instinct to protect our babies is strong. There's no point in bucking Nature!

• **Newborns don't take up a lot of space.** There's usually room for a cradle or bassinet, even in a small bedroom.

• **Young babies are not upset in any way by observing their parents' intimate behavior.** Concerns about babies being present during adult lovemaking probably become realistic only once children are nine months or older (and even then, it's not clear that such scenes are harmful).

Eventually, of course, you'll want to move your baby to her own room. When you do so depends, of course, on how much space you have, how well you can sleep with your baby in your room (it's amazing how much noise these little beings can make in their sleep), and when you feel that your baby is ready for the change.

Many parents choose to make the change when their babies are around three or four months old. At that age, they tend to sleep in long enough blocks so that the parents don't feel as if they're always hopping out of bed to look after them. Making a transition at this age also makes sense from the baby's point of view. A baby who wakes up at night and sees Mommy or Daddy right there is likely to call out or cry until the parent wakes up and makes everything OK. A baby who wakes up alone in her room is more likely to do something to soothe herself. Self-soothing is one of the important skills an infant usually masters around four months of age.

Making the shift to the big-kid bed

When is the right time to switch your child from the crib to a "big-kid" bed? It's certainly time to switch when a child starts being able to climb out of the crib even with the springs in the lowest possible position and the sides all the way up. Often, this is when a toddler reaches 35 or 36 inches in height. Switching to a bed reduces the chances of children being harmed if they fall.

The other reason many parents switch is that there is another baby on the way who will need the crib. It's best to make the switch to a bed before the new baby arrives. For the older child, having a new baby brother or sister means giving up a lot of things, especially the special attention one got from parents by being the youngest, or only, child. To have to give up one's crib, too, is just adding insult to injury. So, if you can arrange the transition to a big-kid bed well before the new baby needs the crib, you can make it easier for your older child to feel OK about making that change.

Just as with everything else, different children handle going from crib to bed in various ways, depending on their temperaments. A child who takes most changes in stride will make the transition easily; a child who has a harder time with change may fuss or have difficulty sleeping. A very active child may take the opportunity to get up out of bed a lot, and you'll need to be quite consistent and firm in setting the limits. Here are some tips to make the transition go more smoothly:

• **Start talking about the new, big-kid bed a few days before you actually get it.** This gives your child time to get excited about the idea. If possible, let him have a hand in picking it out.

• **Position the bed so your child feels secure.** Push the bed into a corner, and use a safety rail for the open side so that your child feels snugly contained.

• **Transfer as much as you can from the crib**. Move the special blanket, pillow, and toys to the new bed so that it has a familiar feel.

• **Let your child select a special set of sheets that will make the bed seem especially wonderful.** It doesn't matter whether or not the sheets are fresh from the store, just that they're pleasing and new to him.

• **When your child tries the bed, let him know you are proud of his growing up.** But don't offer big rewards or make too big a deal of the event. Let his own pride and pleasure be his reward.

• **If your child isn't comfortable for the first few nights, listen to his feelings and accept them.** But still insist, in a kindly way, that the new bed is where he needs to sleep now.

• **Go through your usual bedtime routine.** If your child gets out of bed and comes into your room, be pleasant but firm. Walk him back to his bed, let him know that this is where he needs to be and that you know he'll feel comfortable soon. Your confidence on this point is very important. If you believe that your child will be able to handle sleeping in a new bed, chances are, he will.

• **Even if you are ever so tired, don't give in to the impulse to let your child sleep in your bed "just this once."** Instead, be firm, even if it means walking him back to bed a dozen times a night. After a short while, the nighttime visits to your bedroom will trail off, and you'll all be able to sleep better.

• **Give your child some slack.** While he's adjusting to the new bed, don't be surprised if he does a little back-sliding in such areas as table manners or sharing.

Sleep Supplies

What supplies does your baby need in order to be able to sleep safely and well? The possibilities seem endless: cribs, cradles, bassinets, and newer contraptions called "co-sleepers," playpens, mobiles, monitors, and more. All of these things are attractive, many are expensive, and only a few are really necessary. A couple of common-sense principles can help you choose wisely: First, safety tops the list of priorities. We know a lot about how to keep babies safe while they sleep and play. Second, no piece of equipment, no matter how terrific, can take the place of a loving, responsive parent.

BABY BEDS AND BEDDING

There is something very comforting about being together at night, both for new babies and their parents. You could bring your baby into bed with you, but not all parents like that arrangement. You could bring the baby's crib into your bedroom, but it might be too large to fit, or you may not want to be separated from your newborn by the bars. The traditional solution to this dilemma is to use a cradle or bassinet, a tiny bed that sits next to your own. Co-sleepers are a new option, giving your baby a space that is attached to your bed, but separate. Whichever of these three you choose, all of the same safety rules for cribs apply (see page 59), and there are additional cautions as well.

Cradles and bassinets

Cradles usually rock or swing; bassinets tend to roll (making it easy to settle your baby down to sleep in many different rooms). Otherwise, they are basically the same: comfortable, compact sleeping compartments with sides high enough to prevent your infant from falling out. (For that matter, a sturdy cardboard box or a drawer equipped with a firm, well-fitting pad can serve the same purpose, without any of the expense.) Unless your child is very active, a cradle or bassinet may be all you need for the first two or three months. Be sure it has a wide-enough base so that it won't tip over. Most also come with pins or pegs to keep them from rocking and rolling when you don't want them to. Check the product label to see what the weight limit is. And if you are using an heirloom or secondhand cradle or bassinet, be especially careful to check for sharp edges, splinters, or other hazards.

Co-sleepers

These clever and relatively new devices work like a cradle that attaches to your bed. They have one removable side, making it easy for you to reach your baby in the middle of the night. Be careful that there is no gap between the co-sleeper and your bed that your baby could fall into, and that the co-sleeper is adjusted to the same height as your bed. Co-sleepers may be nice, but they are by no means necessary, and they tend to be a bit pricey. Ones that convert into other pieces of equipment (such as changing tables, for example) might be a better investment.

Cribs

When it comes to selecting a crib, the only truly important features are those that will keep your baby safe (see page 59). Of course, you'll want to find one that also looks nice since you're going to spend many hours gazing at your peacefully sleeping baby—and many more when she's not quite so peaceful! But babies have no eye for style. Your baby will feel at home in any safe crib. There are some practical features worth looking for, however:

• **The side rail should go up and down easily and quietly.** There is nothing quite like settling a baby into a nice, drowsy state only to have her jolted awake by a squeaky crib rail.

• **A rail that can be operated with one hand is convenient, especially when you are carrying a baby or diapers and a damp cloth.**

• **A sturdy crib that doesn't rattle and creak is a blessing when your baby decides to practice gymnastics in the middle of the night.**

• **Metal cribs are sometimes rickety or have sharp spots at the welds, so inspect them carefully before you buy.**

• **Finally, look for cribs that are easy to assemble and don't require a lot of tools.**

A word about convertible cribs: A crib that converts to a toddler bed (see the section on toddler beds on page 66) usually costs more. If you know you'll want a toddler bed later on, it may be a good investment. But if you are planning on having more than one child, you may want to have both a crib and a toddler bed at the same time, or you might decide to do without the toddler bed altogether. Most babies do fine going directly from a crib to a twin bed.

Safety principles for cribs
The Consumer Products Safety Commission (CPSC), the American Academy of Pediatrics (AAP), and other well-regarded organizations have long lists of safety standards and recommendations for cribs, cradles, bassinets, and playpens, as well other baby equipment.

While the sheer number and breadth of the recommendations can be a little intimidating, using a checklist can help (see page 62). Another way to remember the key safety recommendations is to consider the dangers they are meant to prevent. There are lots of recommendations, but only four main sorts of danger—suffocation, strangulation, choking, and falls. And while you probably don't even want to think about such horrible things, understanding the risks is the first step in keeping your baby safe.

Suffocation
Some infants don't have a well-developed gasp reflex. That's the reflex that makes you feel as though you have to have air after you've held your breath too long. A baby without a good gasp reflex may not struggle to breathe if a blanket or other object blocks his airway. For

babies up to 12 months of age, use these guidelines to prevent suffocation:

• **Always put babies to sleep *face up*, lying on their backs.** (See page 6.)

• **Don't put any pillows, stuffed animals, fluffy blankets, or comforters in the crib**. Crib bumpers, those soft pads that are supposed to keep a baby from bonking himself on the wooden sides of the crib, also may pose a suffocation hazard, although the expert recommendations are not clear on this point. It's doubtful that they do much good, in any case, although parents often like the way they look.

• **Use a firm mattress**. Soft, fluffy sleeping surfaces, such as fleeces, feather beds, and waterbeds, can block off a child's breathing more easily than a comfortably firm mattress.

• **Make sure the mattress fits the bed.** If there is more than an inch or so between the mattress and the frame, a baby's face could get caught in the gap, causing suffocation. This is especially a concern with waterbeds, which often have dangerously large gaps between the mattress and the frame.

Strangulation
Babies often don't have the strength or coordination to free themselves if something gets caught around their necks. To prevent strangulation:

• **Be sure that the slats on the crib are no more than 2 3/8 inches apart.** This won't be a problem for any crib you buy new from a U.S. manufacturer. But beware of used cribs. Check, too, that none of the slats are loose, broken, or splintered.

• **Check the size of any cutout designs in the headboard or footboard of the crib.** Make sure that none of these decorative cutouts are greater than 2 3/8 inches in diameter so there's no chance that your baby's head could get stuck in the openings.

• **Make sure the corner posts of the crib don't stick up more than 1/16 of an inch.** Blankets and other cloth items can become caught on corner posts, and then get wrapped around the baby's neck. If the crib has fancy carved corner posts, you may be able to simply unscrew them.

• **Keep mobiles at a distance.** Make sure any mobiles are well out of reach, and remove crib gyms and mobiles once your baby is old enough to sit up.

• **Check the lengths of strings.** If you use a crib bumper or attachable activity center, make sure the ties are short enough so they cannot possibly form a loop 14 inches around or longer.

• **Keep the crib away from windows with cords that hang down from curtains or blinds.** A curious baby can reach out, grab a cord, and become tangled in it.

CRIB SAFETY CHECKLIST

☐ Crib doesn't wobble (all screws and bolts are tight).

☐ There are no sharp edges, splinters, or pieces that can break off.

☐ Slats (or bars) are no more than 2 3/8 inches apart. None are missing, cracked, or loose.

☐ When raised, rails are at least 26 inches higher than the surface the mattress rests on (in lowest position). When lowered, rails are at least 9 inches above the mattress support.

☐ Mattress fits snugly—less than two finger widths between edge of mattress and crib side.

☐ Mattress support is securely attached to the head- and footboards.

☐ Corner posts are no higher than 1/16 inch.

☐ Cutouts in the head- and footboards are small enough so they don't allow head entrapment.

☐ Drop-side latches can be securely locked.

☐ The crib was not made before 1975, unless all the paint has been thoroughly stripped off and replaced to avoid lead-poisoning danger.

Choking

Babies who can't yet hold a rattle still sometimes manage to choke on a huge variety of objects, including buttons, pieces of plastic, pebbles, etc. The safest course is to assume that anything within reach may eventually make it into your baby's mouth and windpipe. To prevent choking:

• **Beware of toys with small parts that could break off, such as teddy bears with button eyes or trucks with loose wheels.** Keep such toys out of the crib. Anything less than $1^3/_4$ inches in diameter is small enough to block off an infant's airway.

• **Check the crib for any splintered plastic** (especially the plastic pieces on the top rails, intended to prevent babies from teething on the wood).

Falls

Babies can get hurt falling from the crib, or if things fall *on* them. To prevent injury from falls:

• **Be careful where you place the crib.** Don't put the crib under a bookshelf, heavy picture, or wall-hanging that could fall down.

• **Make sure the mattress support is firmly attached to the headboard and footboard.** Otherwise, it could slip free and fall. Check to make sure that the crib is sturdy, and that all the screws are tight.

• **Keep the mattress in the proper position.** Once your baby can sit up, lower the mattress as far as it will go and remove any crib bumpers. Sooner or later, he's bound to fall while trying to climb out.

• **Be ready to make the transition to a bed.** Once your baby is 35 inches or taller, or can get a foot up to the rail of the crib, it's time to move to a bed.

Crib bedding options
Although pretty, fashionable bedding in the nursery may give you a warm and cozy feeling, color-coordinated, designer-name sheets, blankets, pillows, and ruffles won't mean a thing to your baby. What *is* important is that the materials feel good and are safe. Here are some practical considerations to consider when deciding what—and what not—to purchase:

• **I am not a fan of ruffles and bumpers, because I feel that, in general, the more cloth surrounding a baby, the**

OLDER CRIBS MAY CONTAIN LEAD PAINT 🐾

Before 1975, most paint contained lead, which, when eaten, can cause anemia and learning and behavior problems. If you have an older crib, be sure that the original paint has been thoroughly stripped off and replaced. Otherwise, don't use the crib!

---

more opportunities for suffocation and exposure to dust mites. (Dust mites are microscopic creatures that make their home in carpeting and cloth. They don't bite, but they shed tiny bits of their shells and feces, which can cause allergies in some people.) If you do use bumpers, be sure to remove them when your baby begins to stand so she can't use them to launch a great escape from the crib.

• **Choose materials that you can launder repeatedly on high heat.** Nylon and other synthetics can melt, and perhaps become a choking hazard.

• **White looks great, but it shows stains well, too.** If you can avoid using chlorine bleach, you may save your baby an uncomfortable rash.

• **Active babies may do a lot of rubbing against the sheets, so choose a smooth, soft material.**

• **Most crib mattresses are plastic covered, so you'll want one or two cloth mattress pads.** A thin pad is fine, and thicker and softer ones may not be as safe.

• **You'll also need at least a couple of fitted sheets, depending on how frequently you plan on doing laundry.**

• **It's helpful to have several receiving blankets on hand**. These small blankets tend to get soiled quickly, and they're useful not only for sleeping, but also for changing and going outdoors.

• **For babies older than 12 months, a comforter or quilt is cozy.** But you need to be careful not to let young babies become overheated, as that increases the risk of SIDS. A blanket sleeper (also known as a sleep sack) or a light blanket and a "onesie" is usually fine, unless your home is chilly.

• **Pillows are not safe in the crib until babies are about one year old, when any risk of SIDS is well past.**

TODDLER, TWIN, AND BUNK BEDS

When your child is ready to move out of her crib—usually sometime between 18 and 36 months—you have lots of choices. Some cribs are made to convert into toddler beds, or you can buy a separate toddler bed. You might be tempted to opt for a bunk bed right away (please see section on bunk beds on page 68 to learn why this isn't the best idea). Or, like most people, you can go straight into a regular twin bed.

Toddler beds vs. twin beds

Toddler beds aren't at all necessary, but they do have their appeal. By the time your child is ready to switch to a big-kid bed, he might be delighted by the idea of having a bed that looks like Noah's Ark or a race car—just two of the designs available today. Although such designs can be fun, a bed that doesn't have a particular theme is more flexible. A plain bed lets your child's imagination, aided by a few props such as extra sheets and pillows, transform it into anything he likes, from a Wild West fort to a medieval castle, a rocket ship to a sailboat.

Toddler beds also have some points in their favor from a practical point of view. They take up less room than twin beds, which can be useful if space is tight in your child's room. It's convenient to be able to use the old crib sheets and mattress for a while, and being surrounded by familiar bedding may help ease a child's transition into a big-kid bed. Many toddler beds come with partial side rails, reducing the risk of a child's tumbling out of bed. Even if they don't have side rails, toddler beds are low to the ground, so there's less concern about falls.

Parent to Parent

"Our toddler fought us at bedtime. The only thing I could think of was that she realized 'UH-OH, I'm not a baby anymore, and maybe I don't like this whole growing-up thing!' Stick to your guns—it's well worth the effort. Independence is one of the most rewarding things we can teach our children."

— **chelsea,** AS POSTED ON DRSPOCK.COM

On the other hand, since your child will soon outgrow his toddler bed, you'll have to move him to a twin bed in the not-so-distant future. This means the toddler bed may not be worth the extra expense. If you're worried about the risk of injury from falls, you can buy sturdy safety rails that fit twin beds—just be sure that the rails are firmly attached, and that there isn't a large gap between the rails and the side of the bed that could trap your child. You also could simply place the twin mattress directly on the floor as a safety precaution.

No matter which type of bed you choose for your toddler, try to limit the number of stuffed animals that accompany him off to dreamland. At this age, the risk of suffocation is greatly reduced, but if allergies or asthma run in your family, stuffed animals are particularly good at harboring dust mites, one of the most common allergen sources.

Bunk beds

Bunk beds are usually reserved for older children, but you may be thinking of buying one for your toddler. Please think again. Bunk beds are great fun for children and they can save space, but they are also notoriously dangerous. Each year, thousands of injuries are reported. Children roll off and break their arms, even with guardrails in place. They topple off the ladders. They get wedged between the top bed and the wall. The top bunks have even been known to come crashing down, sometimes with fatal results. Probably the best advice about bunk beds is, avoid them if you possibly can. If you like the idea of having another bed in the room for sleepovers, a trundle bed (in which a second bed frame and mattress fit under the primary bed and slide out when needed) is a safer option.

OTHER SLEEP SUPPLIES

Playpens and portable play yards
These nifty inventions provide a safe space for babies (and younger toddlers) to sleep and play in. All the safety guidelines for cribs should apply to playpens as well—for example, making sure the mattress fits snugly and is not too soft, avoiding soft pillows and other possible suffocation risks (until a child is about a year old, when the risk of SIDS is virtually zero), being aware of cords or loops of cloth that could be choking hazards, and so on. For playpens with mesh sides, the mesh should be no larger than 1/4 inch across (so that the baby can't get a button or other small part caught in the mesh), and there shouldn't be any tears in the fabric. Not all playpens are as safe and stable as others. Before buying one, it's a good idea to check to see if a particular model has been recalled. You can do this at your local library, or on the Internet at www.cpsc.gov.

Crib toys
Babies spend a fair amount of time awake in their cribs, so it's nice if they can be entertained. A colorful mobile can keep a newborn interested for a long time. Obviously, from a baby's vantage point, a good crib

mobile looks interesting from the bottom, not necessarily from the side, so judge it accordingly. For older infants, crib activity centers (which might feature a row of interesting pictures and textures, buttons and latches that make sounds when pressed, and other diversions) are very popular.

When choosing a mobile (or other attachable crib toy), look out for strings that are longer than a few inches, which might pose a strangulation risk (if they can form a loop more than 14 inches around, they are a danger). Be sure the mobile attaches firmly with clamps, strings, or straps, so it doesn't fall on your baby. And once a baby can sit up or reaches five months of age, it's best to remove any crib mobiles altogether.

Babies love to look around. If you don't use a crib bumper, your baby will be able to see into the room while she's lying on her back—another source of entertainment. Some babies love looking at themselves in a mirror (get one that's unbreakable, of course; they have them in baby-supplies stores). They won't know who that "other" baby is until they are about 18 months old. High-contrast, black-and-white pictures for the crib used to be all the rage. If your baby likes them, that's good. But there isn't any reason to believe that they make babies smarter. And I've seen some babies who are so surrounded by pictures, mirrors, mobiles, and noisemakers that they are thoroughly overwhelmed. One or two interesting objects is all most babies need, or can enjoy, at a single time.

By age three or four months, most babies have discovered their hands and other body parts. For a while, their favorite "toys" are likely to be themselves! By five or six months, once babies can reach, hold, and let go of objects, they get a lot of joy from rattles, small stuffed animals, and books made out of cloth or cardboard. It's wise to keep large, soft pillows or stuffed animals out of the crib. Why tempt fate? Up until your baby is 12 months old, these items increase the risk of SIDS and, after that, bigger toys or objects easily become stepping stools for the adventuresome baby intent on "escaping." (If you use crib bumpers, be sure to remove them when your baby begins to stand, for the same reason.)

Night lights

Night lights may seem convenient and simple, but they can actually be dangerous. Once a child can crawl or scoot, he may make his way to a bright, attractive plug-in night light and grab it. The result can be a burn or a shock. If you opt for the other type of night light—a softly glowing small lamp that sits on a dresser or table—a toddler can tug on the cord and bring the lamp crashing down. Both types are known to cause a number of fires every year, usually after a hot bulb has come into contact with fabric or paper.

Installing a dimmer switch to control the overhead light in your child's room or leaving the hall light on and your child's door partly open probably are safer alternatives. However, if you decide to use a night light, there are several things you can do to make it safer. If you use the plug-in variety, place it only in a wall outlet that is up high and well out of your child's reach. If you use a lamp-type night light, be careful to route the cord behind a heavy piece of furniture so your toddler can't grab it. Keep both types away from drapes, bedding, and other flammable materials. Look for models that bear the mark of a safety-testing laboratory (such as "UL" for Underwriters Laboratories). Finally, you might consider using the new cooler, mini neon bulbs rather than the standard four- to seven-watt bulbs.

Music, vibrations, and white noise
Some babies seem to fall off to sleep more easily sur-rounded by a gentle humming or "white noise." For not too much money, you can buy a white-noise generator. You could also just turn a radio or television to a "static" channel and leave it on low. Vibrators that attach to a crib are advertised as helping children with colic to fall asleep, much like riding in a car, but don't believe claims that this approach is "scientifically proven." On the other hand, it's harmless enough. Soft music might have the same soothing effect. But be aware: If your baby gets used to falling asleep with these sounds or sensations, she may have a very hard time getting to sleep without them, both at bedtime and when she wakes in the middle of the night.

CHAPTER 2

Feeding

"In the first year, feeding is a baby's great joy. She gets her early ideas about life from the way feeding goes. She gets her first ideas about the world from the person who feeds her."

— **Dr. Benjamin Spock,** *Baby and Child Care*

When it comes to feeding a child, there are many different paths to success. One hundred years ago, mothers were taught to keep their babies on a strict schedule. Fifty years ago, experts began to promote the idea of feeding on demand. Now we understand that different babies have different needs. The key to success is not a one-size-fits-all rule, but a flexible approach that changes to fit each individual baby and family.

Successful feeding is a partnership. With a new baby, your part is to offer a breast or bottle at the right time and help your baby to get into position and latch on, burp when needed, and stop when full. Your baby's part is to send clear signals for hunger and fullness, and to let you know what's working and what isn't. Even very young babies are good at communicating this crucial information through their body language and behavior. By paying attention to this feedback, you gradually learn how to make the small, moment-to-moment adjustments that make feeding look like a well-rehearsed dance. Of course, it doesn't always work so smoothly. Sometimes the feedback is that you literally get the feed back! That's usually a sign that your baby has taken too much all at once.

Just as with sleeping, a "good" eater can make a parent feel wonderfully competent. A baby whose hunger cycles are less regular, who responds intensely to bodily discomforts (such as gas), or who has food sensitivities or other chronic illnesses, may make even the most confident parent feel like a failure. After all, as the most elemental of bodily needs, feeding rightfully sits at the heart of the parent-child relationship. But when feeding becomes the entire focus—the principal way a parent expresses love or gives comfort—the result can be a seriously overweight child. You want your child to enjoy food, but to have other interests, as well.

The goal of this chapter is to lay out all the current thinking on this vital topic to help you make choices that are right for your family, from that first big decision about whether to breastfeed or bottle-feed your newborn to devising feeding strategies for a finicky three-year-old. And as you nourish your child from infancy to toddlerhood, remember that one of the most important things about healthy eating is that it feels good. Have fun!

Nutritional Basics

Before I talk about *how* to feed your baby, I'd like to take a moment to explain *what* you should feed her. When you understand a little about the fundamentals of sound nutrition, you are better able to plan a healthy diet for your child and adjust to her changing needs as she grows.

Many nutrients make up a healthy diet

The building blocks of nutrition are proteins, carbohydrates, fats, vitamins, minerals, and water. Proteins are contained in meats, eggs, and fish, and also in many vegetables (mostly legumes) and whole-grain products. Carbohydrates—sugars and starches—come largely from fruits, vegetables, grains, and other plant sources. Fats come from both animal and plant sources. Animal fats are more likely to contribute to heart disease, stroke, and related conditions, and only animal products contain cholesterol.

Proteins, carbohydrates, and fats all provide energy in the form of calories, but ounce for ounce, fats provide roughly twice as many calories as either proteins or carbohydrates. (Low-fat diets aren't necessarily low in calories, of course; two ounces of sugar is about as fattening as one ounce of fat.) Vitamins and most minerals are substances needed in only small quantities for

---

KEY: 🄽 =Newborn (0-2 mos.) 🄱 =Baby (2 mos.-1 yr.) 🅃 =Toddler (1-3 yrs.)

75

healthy functioning. However, growing children need a relatively high amount of two minerals, calcium and iron, because these are key ingredients in bones, muscles, blood, and brain.

In the first six months of life, diets based on breast milk or formula provide a healthy balance of these nutrients. After that, babies learn to eat an increasing variety of foods, and begin to establish preferences. By age two, a healthy toddler's diet looks a lot like a healthy adult's, with a mixture of foods from all groups, lots of whole grains and vegetables, a moderate amount of protein and carbohydrates, and relatively little fat.

Within those broad outlines, there is room for a lot of variety. Children can thrive on vegetarian diets, for example, and even diets that avoid all dairy if the diet is carefully planned to provide all essential nutrients from other sources. (In fact, there is some evidence that such diets might provide long-term nutritional benefits.) On the other hand, there is concern that many U.S. children are eating far too much junk food, rich in processed sugar, salt, and fat, and getting far too little exercise. The resulting rise in obesity and diabetes is a national concern.

Checkups ensure that your baby's well nourished

The main goal of feeding, of course, is to have a baby who is physically healthy. In general, you want a baby who is growing normally, has lots of energy, takes joy in living, and has regular, healthy elimination. It seems as if it should be easy to know if your baby fits this picture of health, but, in fact, it can be surprisingly difficult.

Because you see your baby every day, it's easy to miss small changes that add up over time. As a result, babies can be quite overweight or underweight and their caring and involved parents may simply not notice.

This is not to say that you shouldn't try to watch your baby closely. But in addition to your own observations, it's good to get an objective outside view from time to time. So, the best way to know whether or not your child is getting adequate nutrition is to take him to the doctor's for regular checkups. Your child's healthcare provider has three measuring tools that are vital to gauging growth that you probably don't have at home: an accurate scale, a board for measuring length lying down, and a stadiometer for measuring standing height. (A stadiometer is one of those long vertical measuring sticks with a short horizontal bar that slides down on top of the child's head.) The other necessary tool is a set of national growth charts. With these, the doctor can tell if your child is within the normal range for weight and height (often referred to as the growth curve), and, even more important, whether or not your child's pattern of growth over time is a healthy one.

The hallmark of healthy growth is that a child stays more or less at the same level, relative to other children his age and sex. For example, a nine-month-old boy who weighs 18 pounds is in the 10th percentile for his age, meaning that 10 percent of boys weigh less than he does, and 90 percent weigh more. If the same boy comes back at 12 months weighing 20 pounds, he is still in the 10th percentile. That's a healthy growth pattern. The boy is on the small side, but he is maintaining his own growth curve well, and it's a good bet that he's eating well, too.

Doctors also rely on physical examination to judge a child's nutritional status. They look at skin, hair, and nails; muscle development; and general behavior and appearance. A blood test for iron deficiency is usually done between 6 and 12 months of age. Other tests are done only if there are specific reasons to be concerned.

Feeding and Growth at Different Ages

As children grow, the challenges of feeding change. First, you and your baby have to develop a good breastfeeding partnership, or, if you decide to bottle-feed, you might have to experiment to find the right formula. Just when you've got these basics down pat, it's time to start your infant on solid foods, which introduces a whole new routine. Then there are the issues of weaning from the bottle and dealing with what may seem like constantly changing food likes and dislikes. Understanding how your child's growth and development affect his eating habits makes the whole process a bit less mysterious and will help you deal with the feeding problems that are sure to arise from time to time.

NEWBORNS

Most babies don't feed very well in the first couple of days. A breastfed infant may take a while to figure out how to latch on and suckle, and a brand-new infant given a bottle may take a few sips, lose interest, and fall back to sleep.

In the first week to 10 days of life, it is not unusual for babies to lose a little weight—as much as 5 to 10 percent of their birth weight—before starting to pick up again. Full-term babies are born with enough fat and extra fluid in their bodies to help them get through this initial period. A premature infant may not have as much nutritional padding, and so may need closer watching to make sure she doesn't become dehydrated.

By 5 to 10 days of life, an infant should be growing at a good clip, putting on approximately one ounce per day. This is the fastest a healthy person ever grows once out of the womb. A baby who starts out very large might grow a little more slowly; a baby who is small at birth might grow more quickly for a while, until she catches up to her genetic potential. At one ounce a day, a baby puts on close to half a pound a week.

By about three months, growth slows down a bit, to closer to two ounces every three days or so. Even so, by four months of age, most babies have doubled their birth weight.

From birth to about six months of age, babies don't need any solid food at all. They can thrive very nicely on breast milk or an iron-fortified infant formula. (See pages 83-119 for advantages and details of each feeding method.) Some parents believe that starting solid foods earlier helps babies sleep through the night, but research hasn't backed this up. Many babies are capable of eating solid food when they are three months old or even

79

younger. But getting an earlier start doesn't seem to offer any real advantage, and it does increase the chance that a baby will be overweight. Overweight babies, we now know, often grow into overweight adults, with all of the health problems that entails. Also, infants who eat solid food fill their diapers with larger, smellier bowel movements.

FOUR TO TWELVE MONTHS

Four months is a watershed age in many ways. It's when most babies begin to be able to sleep through the night, and newborn crying and colic are largely past. A four-month-old usually can hold his head up straight, as long as his body is supported. His vision is better, so he begins to take more of an interest in people and things that are across the room, not just what's right next to him. Nutritionally, it's when many parents begin to give their babies solid foods to eat.

Young infants have a reflex response to anything solid put in their mouths. They tend to push it out with their tongues. For most babies, this reflex begins to fade after about three or four months. Before then, trying to feed solids is bound to be an exercise in frustration. Even though many parents start earlier, most babies don't really need to begin solid foods until they are about six months old. The American Academy of Pediatrics recommends breast milk as the only nutrition a baby needs until about six months of age. Commercial formulas also can provide adequate nutrition. Whether you start solids at four, five, or six months probably doesn't make much difference in the long run.

Solid foods provide a number of nutritional advantages. Fortified baby cereals are a good source of iron, which is crucial not only for making blood, but also for the brain and other tissues. Solid foods pack more calories into a small volume, a real advantage for an active child whose need for energy is growing faster than his stomach. Babies who start solids much later than about six months sometimes have a hard time accepting different textures and tastes, so that learning to eat when they are older becomes quite difficult.

Babies are still growing very quickly during this period, although not as fast as during the first three months. A typical baby doubles his birth weight by 4 months, and triples it by 12.

TODDLERS

Until one year of age, your baby can satisfy most of her nutritional needs with breast milk or formula. But as solid foods become a bigger part of her diet, concerns about nutrition tend to increase. Many toddlers have diets that are poor in iron, calcium, and fiber. Struggles over food choice—and how much food gets eaten—are all too common with toddlers. But the second year of life also can be the time that your child discovers a wide range of things she likes, and starts building healthy eating habits that will serve her well throughout her life.

Feeding

Toddlers can eat almost everything—and if you give them a chance, they probably will. Be wary of foods that toddlers can choke on. These include any small, hard, or round foods, and anything that breaks up into chunks that could get lodged in a baby's windpipe. For example, bananas are fine, but grapes are risky, unless you cut them in half. (For a more comprehensive list, see page 125.) The risk of choking never completely goes away, but most five- to six-year-olds are careful enough with their chewing and swallowing to eat all common foods safely.

Somewhere between 9 and 14 months of age, growth slows down for most babies, so that they are gaining, on average, only about one ounce every four days—one quarter as much as when they were newborns. At the same time, many toddlers have a drop-off in appetite, which parents often find alarming. If you notice this happening to your child, it's easy to fall into the trap of pushing your toddler to eat more because her growth has slowed. Unfortunately, toddlers being who they are, the chances are quite good that your child will rebel against your attempt to control what she eats, and will in fact eat less.

A better idea is to check with your child's health-care practitioner. If your toddler is growing well, you may be able to relax about her nutrition. It's best to avoid power struggles that you can't win anyhow. There are several ways you can deal effectively with a finicky toddler, which I'll discuss a little later, but none of them involve trying to push or trick your child into eating when she's not hungry.

Breastfeeding

There are women who never think twice about breast-feeding—they are just absolutely certain that they want to nurse their babies. Others know that bottle-feeding is for them and never seriously consider breast-feeding. But most women think long and hard about the decision. If you are in this position, you need as much information on the topic as you can get. The goal of this section is not to "sell" you on breastfeeding or bottle-feeding, but to help you arrive at the decision that is right for you.

Benefits of breastfeeding to babies and mothers

There is no question that breast milk beats infant formula as far as nutrition goes. All female mammals make milk, but the recipe, so to speak, is different from species to species. Human breast milk is the perfect food for baby humans, and cow's milk is the perfect food for baby cows.

In fact, human babies fed straight cow's milk tend to become quite ill. The proportion of nutrients is all wrong. To make cow's milk acceptable for human babies, it has to be processed to change the fat, protein, iron, and salt content. The result is infant formula. Babies are able to digest formula well enough, but it is not the same as human milk.

Human milk contains just the right proportions of protein, fats, sugars, and salt that babies need. There are many other benefits as well.

❝

• **Protection against infections.** Breast milk may help protect babies against some common infections that cause diarrhea and vomiting, as well as infections in the ear, nose, sinuses, and lungs. It's not clear from the research how long a mother needs to breastfeed to pass on these health benefits, but, most likely, even breastfeeding for a short time offers at least some of these advantages. In fact, although longer is probably better, the very first weeks and months may be the most important of all.

• **Protection against food allergies.** Exposure to allergens early in life is one of the main causes of allergies. Many infants develop allergies to the proteins in formula made from cow's milk or soy. But allergies to human milk are unheard of. Some researchers believe that babies who are exclusively breastfed for six months or more may have lower rates of allergies to many other foods, as well.

• **Less obesity.** Breastfed infants tend to be leaner than bottle-fed ones, particularly in the second half of the first year. Some experts believe that they have a lower risk of becoming obese later in life.

• **Less risk of diabetes.** According to some research studies, breastfed infants may have a lower risk of developing autoimmune diseases, which occur when the immune system attacks the body itself. Among these are juvenile-onset diabetes, multiple sclerosis, and two serious diseases affecting the intestines, Crohn's disease and ulcerative colitis.

• **Improved brain development (higher IQ).** Several studies show that babies who were breastfed have higher IQs. But the scientific jury is still out as to whether or not the breast milk itself is the cause. Breast milk does contain substances that may be important for brain development; most formulas do not. The brain-enhancing effects of breast milk may be most important for premature infants who are at higher risk of later learning problems.

Moms benefit, too

Babies aren't the only ones who benefit from breast-feeding. There are many health advantages to mothers who breastfeed, as well. These include:

• **Weight loss.** Breastfeeding uses up a lot of calories, helping nursing mothers to return to their pre-pregnancy weights more quickly.

• **Quicker shrinking of the uterus, with less bleeding.** During breastfeeding, the brain releases a hormone called oxytocin, which has several positive effects. It causes the uterus to contract, and thus to bleed less while your body recovers from childbirth.

Q: *Does breast milk contain all the nutrients my baby needs early in life?*

A: *Breast milk alone contains everything your baby needs up to six months of age, with one exception: Dark-skinned babies and those exposed to very little sunlight should get extra vitamin D, as prescribed by their doctor. And after six months, babies might need to be given fluoride drops (see page 120). They also may need extra iron, and adding iron-fortified foods such as baby cereals to their diet will take care of this important mineral.*

• **Psychological benefits.** Oxytocin also brings feelings of happiness and contentment, feelings that many mothers report during breastfeeding. (Maybe it's no coincidence that oxytocin also is released during sexual orgasm.)

• **Birth control.** While mothers are breastfeeding, the hormones released act as a form of birth control for at least six months. This effect is not 100 percent foolproof, however, so it's also wise to use other forms of birth control.

• **Lower risk of cancer.** Women who breastfeed also may have lower risks of developing breast cancer and cancer of the ovaries.

Practical pros and cons

One advantage of breast milk that not many mothers consider is cost. The cost of formula over a baby's first 12 months averages about $800. Breastfeeding mothers need to eat a bit more than they would otherwise, but the cost of this added food has been estimated at $400 a year. So there's a real savings here.

Another obvious advantage of breast milk is that the milk is there when you need it. You never have to stand in the kitchen in the middle of the night mixing formula. If you pump your breast milk for later use, you still have to clean bottles and latex nipples, but far fewer than if you were exclusively bottle feeding. When you're away from home, you don't need to take along bottles, formula, and extra nipples. And you don't have to be concerned about your baby taking in germs from unclean water used to mix the formula.

There are obvious practical disadvantages to breast-feeding, as well. Unless you can be with your baby full time—a luxury that fewer and fewer mothers have—you'll need to pump your breast milk to keep your flow up. Pumping is not difficult, but it requires equipment (see page 136). If you are away at work, you'll have to find a private spot where you can feel comfortable pumping. Breastfeeding mothers need certain equipment and supplies, such as nursing bras and pads, described more fully later on in this chapter. Finally, it takes physical energy to produce milk; a nursing mother may have less stamina to do other things, such as work at home or at an office.

Breastfeeding and work

The demands of work outside the home place great pressure on women to stop breastfeeding early, or not to start at all. Although the federal Family Medical Leave Act guarantees that women can take up to 12 weeks of unpaid leave—far less time than in many other developed countries—a lot of women feel that they simply can't afford to lose that much time from work. Mothers who know that they have to return to work soon after delivery may decide not to even start breastfeeding, because the prospect of having to stop soon is so discouraging.

Women in the workplace often face huge barriers if they choose to continue to breastfeed. Among these are lack of privacy and time to pump, fear of embarrassing leakage, painful engorgement, and pressure from colleagues to devote their full energies to the job. Despite

HOW BREAST MILK FIGHTS INFECTION

Babies' immune systems are immature for months after birth. Infections early in life are particularly worrisome, since young babies often get sicker faster than more mature ones.

Breast milk contains many substances that act on different germs, attacking them directly or preventing them from attaching to a baby's cells. Substances in breast milk also stimulate the growth of good bacteria in the infant's intestines, making it harder for harmful bacteria to thrive. Still other components have a control function, ensuring that the different parts of the baby's disease-fighting system work together well. Altogether, there are more than 1,000 different components in human milk, many of which may play a role in fighting infection.

these difficulties, many women do figure out solutions. In some companies, on-site child care allows mothers to take periodic breaks to breastfeed. Other mothers manage to pump their breasts during the workday, and continue to breastfeed the rest of the time. Having a high-efficiency, double-barreled electric pump can help.

Another solution is to stop breastfeeding and expressing milk during the day, using infant formula for the midday feeds and perhaps nursing more frequently at night. While this works for some mothers, others find that they are too engorged and uncomfortable during the day, or that their milk production drops off so much that they don't make enough to satisfy their babies when they are at home. Often, these women stop breastfeeding altogether. Different solutions are right for different women. What's important is that you have thought through all your options, and are honest with yourself about what really matters to you.

PARENT TO PARENT
"One thing that helped get my husband to be completely on board with my breastfeeding was taking him to a breastfeeding class offered at our hospital. The class had as many men as women so he did not feel alone. He paid such great attention to the different positions and so forth that he became my biggest breastfeeding helper. And when his mom expressed her disapproval of my breastfeeding, he let her know he was behind me all the way!"

— **evesmom,** AS POSTED ON DRSPOCK.COM

Breastfeeding and sexuality

Look at almost any television show, or magazine: Breasts are everywhere, selling everything from cars to cleansers. A huge industry in the United States banks on women's breasts' being seen in a sexual light, rather than as a part of women's reproductive and child-nurturing equipment. Of course, breasts are both. But the media focus on the sexual side makes it hard for many women to think of their breasts in any other way. As a result, questions about breastfeeding get all mixed up with issues of sexuality.

Does breastfeeding make breasts unattractive? Many women worry, for example, that breastfeeding will cause their breasts to become droopy or ugly. But changes in breast shape are more related to pregnancy itself than to breastfeeding. Breasts grow during pregnancy, as milk-producing tissues develop. This stretches the fiber support tissue of the breast. Whether or not these tissues spring back once the breasts shrink again is mostly a matter of luck—some women's breasts are springier than others'. Women with highly elastic breasts can breastfeed and, a few months later, look the same as they did before getting pregnant. Other mothers who do not breastfeed can have long-lasting changes in breast shape from their pregnancies.

Does breastfeeding make women unattractive to their husbands or partners? This varies from person to person. Some men are put off by nursing breasts, but many find them interesting and attractive. The fact that their spouse is feeding their baby from her own body fills some men with awe, others with lust. Some nursing mothers feel that their breasts are less sensitive to erotic stimulation. Others find that having larger breasts makes them feel more sensual.

Is breastfeeding sexually arousing? Nursing mothers often report that breastfeeding feels good, but the feeling is not really sexual. It's clear to them that their breasts have developed a specialized function as a source of nutrition for their babies.

Will breastfeeding make your partner feel excluded or jealous? This does happen sometimes, but it doesn't have to. Fathers can help make their partners comfortable for nursing, and they can take over many other parenting tasks, such as changing, holding, singing to, and playing with the baby. Many nursing mothers pump their breast milk regularly, especially if they are working outside of the home, and fathers can certainly feed this to their babies using a bottle, spoon, or cup.

Get support from the beginning

While you're still pregnant, it's a good idea to discuss your breastfeeding plans with your obstetrician. This can be particularly important if you have any reason to believe that breastfeeding is going to be difficult for you, such as:

• **Previous breast surgery.** If you have had surgery to either reduce or enlarge your breasts, there is a chance that this could interfere with their ability to make and deliver milk. This is particularly so if the surgical incision was around the nipple, where the milk ducts run. Biopsies and operations to remove lumps generally don't cause a problem. But it's always better to ask if you are at all concerned.

• **Retracted or flat nipples.** Babies need to be able to latch onto the nipple in order to breastfeed. If your nipples are deeply dimpled or flat, there are often things that can be done to shape them up for feeding.

• **Very large or very small breasts.** Usually this is not a problem, but women who have tube-shaped breasts may have difficulty breastfeeding. And if your breasts have not enlarged noticeably during pregnancy, it may be a sign that the milk-producing glands have not developed. Ask your obstetrician if you are concerned about the size of your breasts.

Check out your hospital's policies
If you decide that you're going to breastfeed, be sure that the hospital at which you'll deliver will:

• **Give you your baby right away.** Right after birth, unless they are ill or have been knocked out by their mothers' pain medication, babies tend to be wide-awake and ready to socialize and nurse. Plenty of babies who never do this still breastfeed perfectly well. But this is a special opportunity to get the nursing started in a very positive direction.

• **Allow your baby to stay with you full time.** Not surprisingly, new babies nurse more often when they are with their mothers more of the time. And the more often newborns nurse, the sooner the mother's milk supply comes in.

• **Avoid giving your baby formula or water.** Up to age six months, healthy babies don't need anything except breast milk. Breast milk is 87 percent water, so a nursing baby gets plenty of water, even in a hot climate. Giving formula or water early on makes babies less hungry for breast milk. Of course, if there is a medical reason why your baby needs supplemental fluids, then by all means he should have them. Your child's healthcare practitioner will let you know if this is the case.

CLASSIC SPOCK
"I think there is one main reason that so many American women stop breastfeeding early: The mother here who is trying to breastfeed, instead of feeling that she is doing the most natural thing in the world and assuming that she'll succeed like everyone else, feels that she's attempting to do the unusual, the difficult thing."

— Dr. Benjamin Spock, *Baby and Child Care*

• **Provide expert breastfeeding teaching.** Unless you are already an experienced breastfeeder, you'll almost certainly benefit from hands-on teaching by a lactation educator. Books and videotapes can help, but there's really no substitute for being shown and reassured by a knowledgeable person.

• **Let you stay until breastfeeding is well established, or send a home visitor.** It usually takes several days—sometimes as long as four or five—before a mother's breast milk comes in well. Most insurance plans won't let mothers stay in the hospital that long (and you probably don't want to, anyway). The next best thing is to have a home visit by a nurse or lactation specialist who can assess how your breastfeeding is going, and offer help if it's needed.

Practical tips
• **It takes time to get started.** Many new moms are surprised to learn that the first fluid their breasts produce isn't milk, it's colostrum. This is a yellowish fluid rich in protein, antibodies, and immune cells that's easy for newborn babies to digest. At two to five days, the colostrum begins to change, increasing in volume and fat content. By about 10 to 14 days, your breasts should be producing a good supply of mature milk. In addition, many babies need two or three days to get the hang of latching on and suckling. A full-term baby can manage well with very little actual nutritional intake for the first couple of days, but breastfeeding should be going well by the fifth day or so.

95

• **Use it or lose it.** The law of supply and demand for breast milk is that the greater the demand, the more your breasts will supply. The flip side is that once you stop emptying your breasts, it does not take long for them to slow down and eventually stop making milk. So the best way to ensure a good milk supply is to make sure your baby feeds often and well.

• **Alternate breasts.** Each breast is independent of the other. If your baby always nurses more from one breast, that breast will make more milk and the other will dry up. To keep things more even, alternate which breast you give your baby first.

• **Keep an eye on the time.** Babies usually will empty a breast in 10 to 15 minutes. A whole feeding might take 20 to 30 minutes. Ask the doctor if your baby is much slower than this or seems to tire out easily during feedings.

• **Take care of yourself, and don't be afraid to ask for help.** Breastfeeding makes many demands on your body. You'll need to eat more (see page 98) and rest more, too. Ask your spouse (or partner) and other family members for help with household chores. And if you're having trouble getting into a smooth breast-feeding routine with your infant, be sure to consult with a lactation expert.

Key signs of breastfeeding success

By the time your baby is a week old, breastfeeding ought to be going well. If it isn't, then you need to ask for help right away, not wait until problems get worse. Signs that breastfeeding is going well include:

• **You have a good "let-down" reflex—a tingling feeling when ducts within the breast contract to expel the milk.** If you have a particularly strong let-down, milk might actually squirt out, much to your baby's surprise.

• **Your baby empties your breasts, nursing for 10 minutes or longer.** Your breasts should feel full before a feeding, and comfortably empty afterwards.

• **When your baby nurses, you hear swallowing sounds.** After nursing, your baby is full and satisfied.

• **Your baby should be having six or more wet diapers a day, and at least four stools that are mustard colored, thin, and dappled with little white specks.**

• **Your baby should be feeding every two to three hours during the day, and at least two or three times during the night (a total of eight or more feedings in a 24-hour period).** A breastfed baby should not sleep through the night.

• **Your baby is active and happy when awake.**

• **You feel comfortable that breastfeeding is going well.**

It's very important that you ask for help if any of the items on the list are not as they should be. Early problems with breastfeeding do happen, and they only tend to get worse unless steps are taken to correct them. A baby who does not get enough to drink can become quite ill in a short time. So if there is any reason you feel that your breastfeeding may not be succeeding, it's very important that you get help from your baby's doctor early, and don't wait until the first scheduled baby visit.

Your diet during breastfeeding

You don't have to drink milk to make milk, but you do need a good intake of water, calcium, protein, vitamins, and roughage in order to stay healthy while supplying your baby's nutritional needs. A nursing mother needs about 500 extra calories a day, which actually isn't a lot of food. If you really do "eat for two," as the saying goes, chances are that you'll gain a lot of unwelcome weight.

Concentrate on eating food of high quality, such as plenty of vegetables and fruits. Lean meats are a good source of iron, zinc, and other minerals. Dark green leafy vegetables are good sources of fiber as well as iron. Dairy products are fine, but cow's-milk proteins pass into breast milk and can cause an allergic reaction. If you suspect this is causing a problem with your baby, try other calcium-fortified foods or juices. Antacid pills that contain calcium are another good source, as are the soft-candy-type chews with calcium and vitamins D and K.

Some foods to avoid: Coffee, colas, and chocolate all contain caffeine, which can make babies irritable. (On the other hand, a *little* chocolate may be a vital necessity of life for you, and is not likely to do any harm.)

Alcohol does pass into breast milk, and any more than very light alcohol use is probably not a good idea. Highly flavored or spicy foods can impart a flavor to your milk. Many babies actually like the taste of garlic, but hot peppers may make your milk unpalatable.

Common breastfeeding problems

When problems arise in breastfeeding, it's good to have a source for answers you trust. Your child's doctor should be well versed in breastfeeding and ready with referrals to lactation specialists. Breastfeeding support groups, such as La Leche League International, are also often good sources of advice. Here are some of the more common problems, along with advice on how to deal with them:

• **Delayed milk production.** It's normal for a brand-new mom to make only a small amount of colostrum, the first yellowish milky substance. But by day three or four, a woman's regular breast milk usually comes in and the volume increases. If this doesn't happen, talk with your baby's doctor. You may need to supplement your breast milk with a bit of formula while your body catches up. Using a breast pump often stimulates milk production, especially for babies who don't suck vigorously at first.

• **Sore, cracked nipples.** Gently rub a moisturizer, such as 100 percent lanolin, on your nipples. Wash your nipples with water only; soap is too drying. Let nipples air-dry when you can. Make sure that your baby is latching on properly, with the whole areola (dark-colored area) in the mouth, not just the nipple. When she's done feeding or you need to change breasts, break the suction by inserting your finger alongside the nipple before pulling it out of your baby's mouth. Sometimes a yeast infection (known as thrush) is to blame for sore, cracked nipples. Check your baby's mouth, looking for white patches in the mouth or a white coating on the tongue. Treatment of your nipples and your baby's mouth with a prescription medication can help.

• **Poor milk supply.** If this happens to you, it usually means that your baby is not taking enough to properly stimulate milk production—remember the law of supply and demand. Try pumping after each feeding to completely empty your breast. Make sure that you are drinking enough water (one to two quarts per day). Get help at home, so you can rest more. There are also medications that can increase milk supply. The longer you go with poor supply, the harder it is to increase it, so it's a good idea to seek help from a lactation consultant or doctor sooner rather than later.

• **Breast engorgement.** Often the cause is the same as poor milk supply—that is, your baby isn't taking enough to empty the breasts. Pumping is the main remedy. Relaxing for a few minutes with a warm cup of herb tea or soothing music can help your let-down reflex work better. A warmed, damp towel placed over the breasts or a warm shower can help as well. Expressing a little milk before feeding can soften the breasts, making feeding easier. Also, try feeding more frequently. Call your doctor if the problem continues for more than a day.

• **Leaking.** This is usually a sign that you have a good milk supply. Breast pads worn inside a nursing bra can help keep clothing dry.

• **Pain, fever, and unusual tiredness.** These can be signs of breast infection (mastitis). This is a serious condition that needs treatment right away. Your doctor probably will prescribe oral antibiotics to cure the infection.

Weaning from the breast
You don't have to stop breastfeeding when your baby reaches a certain age. The American Academy of Pediatrics recommends that women breastfeed through one year of age, and as long after that as they wish. Some mothers choose to continue to nurse their children once or twice a day for years, and these children do fine. If you love the close physical and emotional connection that comes with nursing, there is no reason you have to give it up entirely when your baby turns one.

• **Mixing breast and bottle.** Although breast milk works well as the only nutrition up to six months of age, most mothers end up supplementing with formula earlier than that. Many babies do fine taking both breast and bottle, although some develop the dreaded "nipple confusion," refusing to nurse once they've realized how easy it is to suck milk from a bottle. To prevent this difficulty, it's wise to give your baby at least six weeks of solid breastfeeding before introducing a bottle.

A baby who loves to nurse at the breast might refuse to take a bottle at first. To help make this transition easier for your infant, you might want to introduce one bottle a day, starting at about two months of age (early, but still after your nursing has been well established). When it comes time to wean your baby to a bottle, you simply substitute a bottle for one feeding at a time, usually starting with the feeding when your baby seems the least hungry. It's easiest to do this gradually, switching one bottle for one breastfeeding every two to three days or so, until he is completely weaned. You should let your own comfort level, and your baby's, determine how fast you go with this process.

• **Weaning an older baby.** If your baby is nine months or older, you may want to wean directly from the breast to a cup. Up to one year, however, remember to put infant formula, not regular milk, in the cup. Another tip: Have the father or some other adult help out with weaning to a cup. Babies may be more prone to reject formula or cow's milk when their preferred source (mom's breasts) is right in front of them.

I've been talking about weaning as though it were just a practical challenge. But for many mothers and babies, weaning also has emotional significance. It can feel like losing a special, loving bond. Learning to enjoy feeling connected in different ways—sharing food, play, picture books, and cuddling—is just as important as learning how to swap one form of nutrition for another.

Bottle-feeding

Bottle-feeding your baby may be a choice that you make, or it may be your only option. Either way, it's good to know that infant formulas can provide perfectly adequate nutrition for babies. Yes, breast milk offers some benefits that formula can't match (see page 83), but it's important not to exaggerate them. Most babies reared on formula grow up to be quite healthy, at least in developed countries like the United States, where most families have access to clean water and adequate amounts of formula.

In the past, women who chose to breastfeed were criticized for being backward and unscientific. Nowadays, women who choose to bottle-feed may be criticized for being uncaring, because they are denying their babies the benefits of breast milk. Both of these attitudes are uncalled for. The choice to breastfeed or bottle-feed has nothing to do with how well you love your baby. Feeding your baby is an important part of your life, but you have to be able to balance the demands on your time and energy. Most important, you need to feel comfortable with your choice.

Although most women are capable of breastfeeding, there are some medical conditions that make breastfeeding difficult, impossible, or unadvisable. For example, some women have infections or need to take medications that can pass into the breast milk and make their babies ill (common over-the-counter pain relievers are quite safe). If you take any medication, be sure to ask your doctor whether it is safe to breastfeed. Surgery on the breasts can interrupt the ducts that carry milk to the nipple. Tubular-shaped breasts and small breasts that fail to enlarge during pregnancy may not produce enough milk. (Small breasts that do enlarge during pregnancy make just as much milk as larger breasts, however.)

Economic reality also prevents many women from nursing their babies for as long as they would like; there's no doubt that going back to work can make it hard to keep breastfeeding. Whether bottle-feeding is a choice or a necessity, you should feel confident that your baby can thrive and grow, both physically and emotionally. Breastfeeding can be lovely, but it is not magic. You can communicate love and nurture your baby just as well while holding a bottle.

Advantages of bottle-feeding
Although breastfeeding advocates sometimes are reluctant to admit it, bottle-feeding has certain advantages:

• **Both mother and father can do it.** Feeding a baby is a deeply satisfying experience that fosters bonding. Babies can easily learn to take a bottle from more than one person. In a modern family, mother, father, and perhaps another caregiver might all take an active role in feeding.

• **It's easy to tell how much your baby is getting.** There is something reassuring about being able to actually measure how much formula your baby takes in at any given feeding.

• **Feeding in public may feel more comfortable if you use a bottle.** Although it shouldn't be this way, the fact is that breastfeeding in public can be embarrassing or make others feel rather uncomfortable—at least in our American culture.

• **Feeding formula makes returning to work easier.** Although many women manage to find time and space during the workday to pump their breasts, this is often quite difficult, if not impossible. Bottle-feeding solves this problem.

Choosing a formula

It may seem complicated, but choosing a formula for your baby is actually pretty easy. Most formulas are made from cow's milk or from soybeans. You can use powder, concentrate, ready-to-feed, or some combination of the three. It doesn't matter what brand you choose, as long as you stick to the larger, nationally known ones; there aren't any important nutritional differences. Be sure the formula is fortified with iron—low-iron formula is never a good choice. Iron in formula does not cause constipation, but too little iron in the diet can cause anemia, as well as permanent learning problems.

Cow's-milk formula

This is the standard infant formula. To make it, the manufacturer takes out the butterfat in cow's milk and replaces it with vegetable oil, changes the protein so that there is less casein (curd) and more whey, reduces the salt, increases the sugar, and adds iron and the appropriate vitamins. After all these changes, formula supplies roughly the same amount of calories, protein, sugar, and fat as human milk.

Of course, human milk changes in composition from day to day, most rapidly during the first weeks of a baby's life. It also includes hormones, antibodies, and other components that formula lacks. Remarkably, perhaps, most babies in the United States do well without all of those "extras." In less-developed countries, the advantages of breast milk are much more dramatic and critical. But even in developed countries, there are some experts who believe that cow's milk in any form poses health risks to babies and children. I'll examine that controversy in more detail below, but the bottom line is that the vast majority of nutritionists and pediatricians recommend cow's-milk formula as the way to go for most babies who are bottle-fed.

Soy-based formulas

To make soy-based formulas, the manufacturer starts out with soy protein and adds vegetable oils, salt, and sugar. The end product supplies roughly the same amount of calories, protein, fat, and salt as human milk or cow's-milk formula does. The main difference is that the protein is soy protein, and the sugar is sucrose rather than lactose. Soy formulas are useful for children who cannot digest lactose. Some children who are allergic to cow's-milk protein do well with soy protein, but many children who are allergic to one are allergic to both (see page 116).

Elemental formulas

These formulas are called elemental because instead of using whole soy or cow's-milk proteins, they use mixtures of amino acids (the "elements" out of which proteins are made). The sugar in this type of formula is sucrose, and the fats are either vegetable oils or special highly digestible oils. These formulas are designed for children who are allergic to cow's-milk and soy proteins, or who have special digestive problems. They're very expensive, and they result in unusually smelly bowel movements. Otherwise, they are nutritionally similar to the other formulas. Elemental formulas are wonderful for children who need them, and of no benefit at all for children who don't.

Other formulas

There are many variations on these main themes, as well as special formulas for children with particular medical conditions. Some cow's-milk formulas are made with sucrose instead of lactose. There also are partially elemental formulas that suit some children who can't take regular formulas, but don't need fully elemental ones, either. Let your child's doctor point you in the direction of these special formulas if need be. A few words of warning: If you are considering feeding your child goat's milk, be sure to check with her doctor first because you will need to give your baby special supplements. Finally, formulas made at home from condensed milk are not safe for young babies. They often cause anemia, bleeding into the intestines, and other problems.

Premixed, concentrate, or powder

From your baby's point of view, it doesn't matter whether you use premixed formula, concentrate, or powder. They all have the same nutritional value, and taste pretty much the same. You can mix and match. But do keep the following points in mind:

• **Premixed formula.** This is ready-to-use: Just open the can and pour. It's also the most expensive and the bulkiest to carry home from the store. The single-serving size is handy for car trips or other occasions when you don't have easy access to water and refrigeration. If you use this type, you may also need to give your baby fluoride (see page 120).

• **Concentrate.** To use this type of formula, mix one can of concentrate with one can of water. The usual size, 13 ounces, mixes up to be 26 ounces, which is roughly what an average baby takes in one day. One word of caution: Be sure to mix in one can of water, no more, and no less. If you forget to mix in the water, the formula will be much too concentrated, and it will make your baby sick. If you mix in too much water, your baby will be undernourished and won't grow well. He also could get very ill. A mistake now and then won't do any harm, but using too much or too little water on a regular basis is dangerous.

• **Powder.** This is the least expensive way to buy formula and the easiest to carry home from the store. You can take packets of powder with you and always have formula as long as there is a source of clean water. Be sure to follow the mixing instructions on the package and use the measuring spoon included with the formula. As with concentrate, you have to be careful to use the right amount of powder and water, or your baby could become seriously ill. If you are unsure, ask your child's doctor to show you. Once you get the hang of it, however, mixing the formula will become second nature.

Preparing and storing formula
• **Don't bother boiling the water.** If your tap water comes from a reliable municipal processing plant, you don't need to boil the water—it's clean enough from the faucet. If you have questions about the quality of your water, you can boil it for 10 minutes or, even better, use bottled water. You'll need to use boiled or bottled water for cleaning the bottles and nipples, as well.

• **Use cold water.** Water from the hot tap is more likely to pick up lead from the pipes or the joints between the pipes. Not all homes have lead in their pipes, of course, but it's hard to know for sure. If you run the cold water for a couple of minutes, until it comes out really cold, you're drawing water from the water main, which is lead free. Boiling is not an answer for lead. Boiling water only increases the lead content because the water boils off while the lead remains.

• **Serve formula warm or cold.** Some babies prefer their formula at refrigerator temperature; some like theirs warmed. It makes no difference, healthwise. If you do warm up the bottle, though, be sure to check that the formula is not too hot. A drop placed on your wrist should be just slightly warm.

• **Don't warm up formula in the microwave.** Because microwaves don't heat evenly, they can create hot spots within the milk that can scald your baby even if the bottle itself feels cool. One solution is to make sure to mix or shake the formula after warming it. But this is an easy step to forget. It's safer simply to avoid the microwave.

• **Discard half-finished bottles.** Once a baby has sucked on a bottle, the milk in it contains bacteria from the baby's mouth. If you set the bottle aside to use later, you're giving those germs an opportunity to multiply. It's safer to toss the unfinished formula away and start fresh with a new bottle the next time.

• **Use up any opened formula in a day or two.** Formula is a great place for bacteria to thrive. Once a can is opened, it's best to use its contents up fast, even when the formula is stored in the refrigerator. And if the formula is at room temperature, it can spoil in a matter of hours.

• **Wash bottles thoroughly, but you don't need to sterilize.** Hand-washing with soap and hot water is probably fine. Bottles don't have to be completely germ free, just clean. Most dishwashers do a good job (sometimes too good, melting plastic bottles). Sterilizing is important only if you know your water supply is contaminated, or if your baby has an immune deficiency.

How often, and how much?

A flexible schedule usually is best. Feeding works best when your baby is hungry, but not too hungry. This happens naturally when you and your baby are on roughly the same schedule. One way to get in sync is to follow the clock. If you offer a bottle every four hours, your baby will adjust to that rhythm and feel hungry about every four hours.

This plan works well most of the time, with two exceptions. The first exception is babies who have highly variable hunger cycles. Sometimes they get hungry in two hours, and sometimes they don't get hungry for five or six. A baby's rhythms are inborn. Some babies simply have a much harder time than others staying on a schedule.

If your baby is one of these irregular eaters, it's a mistake to try to stick to a rigid feeding schedule. If you do, you can be sure that a lot of the time your baby won't be hungry when you pop a bottle into his mouth, and at other times he'll be screaming with hunger long before the schedule calls for a bottle. Either way, the result is a cranky baby, an upset stomach, and often vomiting or diarrhea. If you have a baby whose inborn temperament makes it very hard to adjust to your schedule, you need to be flexible enough to adjust to his.

The other time that a very strict feeding schedule won't work is when your baby has a growth spurt and suddenly becomes much hungrier than usual for a couple of days. Little growth spurts happen predictably, about every two weeks, with larger spurts about every two months. If your baby seems ravenous all of a sudden, the sensible thing to do is to feed him, not to stick to an arbitrary schedule.

Flexibility is important, but that's not to say that you should feed your baby completely at his whim. First of all, this makes it hard to plan any activity. Second, feeding entirely on demand doesn't give your baby the chance to develop important self-soothing and waiting skills. If he fusses two hours after finishing a large bottle, it's reasonable to try to distract him with play or conversation, or even by helping him find a finger to suck. (Sucking without getting fed is called non-nutritive sucking, and it's a perfectly normal activity for a baby.) But if that same baby is crying vigorously after three hours, it doesn't make sense to make him wait the full four before satisfying his hunger.

Let your baby decide how much to take. It's healthy to eat when he's hungry, and stop when he's full. Still, many teenagers and adults struggle to exercise this basic self-control. They eat when they are angry, or sad, or celebrating. They diet, ignoring their hunger, then binge past the point of being stuffed.

Healthy self-control starts in infancy. You can help your baby pay attention to his body's own hunger and fullness signals by using the words "hungry," "full," and "more" to describe what you think your baby is feeling. You don't need to respond to all fussing with a bottle, of course. But when your baby does have a bottle, let him decide how much formula to take. Over time, your child will learn to trust his body sensations as a guide for when to eat and when to stop; he'll also come to trust that food will be there when he needs it, but won't be forced on him when he doesn't. These are important and comforting lessons.

When parents try to push or cajole their babies to eat more, the babies have to decide, Do I listen to Mommy and ignore how my body feels, or do I listen to my body and make Mommy mad? It's an awful choice. Over time, many babies learn to eat to please their parents, or they learn not to eat in order to assert their independence.

Letting your child decide how much to take means that sometimes he might drink only two or three ounces, while at other meals he'll want a full eight or more. A child whose inborn hunger cycle is more regular will stick to more or less the same amount each feeding. A less regular child won't have such a predictable intake of food. Nutritionally speaking, both styles of eating are equally healthy. And both can help your child grow up with a healthy relationship to food and to his own body.

Practical tips
• **Get comfortable.** Babies are very sensitive to the moods of the adults who care for them. If you are relaxed, your baby will be, too. Many young babies prefer a quiet place with dim lighting. Premature babies often do better with less stimulation, especially when they are concentrating on eating.

FEEDING

• **Focus on your baby.** In many ways, bottle-feeding can be every bit as much of a close personal interaction as breastfeeding is. Hold your baby so that you can make eye-to-eye contact. Talk softly to your child. Find a quiet room without television or loud music. If you have other children, you may not be able to avoid distractions entirely, of course. But older children can learn that feeding time is not the time to make demands that can wait for a few minutes.

• **Hold the bottle still.** For some reason, many parents jiggle the bottle a lot while they feed. This isn't necessary, and in some cases I think it actually distracts the baby. It's hard to suck milk out of something that keeps moving around!

• **Burping is optional.** Although this comes as a surprise to many parents, not all babies need to burp. Many infants burp on their own. Sometimes just sitting a baby up on your lap for a couple of minutes, halfway through a bottle, is enough to bring out a burp. Or you can gently rub your baby's back. Patting vigorously doesn't really help. Over the shoulder is another good burping position. If you put a diaper over your shoulder first, you won't have to go through the day smelling quite so much like baby-burp.

• **A bottle should last about 10 to 20 minutes.** Much slower than that and your baby probably is working too hard. Much quicker, and your baby is likely to spit a large amount back.

Common bottle-feeding problems

• **Spitting up or vomiting.** A little spitting up is normal. A lot of spitting up, with other signs of discomfort such as crying or arching the back, can be a sign of baby heartburn, or gastroesophageal reflux (see page 189). Smaller, more frequent feedings may help, and your baby's doctor can suggest other things to try.

• **Diarrhea.** Bottle-fed babies usually have bowel movements that are like soft clay in consistency. If they are unusually large and loose, it could be a sign of an intestinal infection (usually accompanied by fever or other signs of illness) or simply overeating. If your baby seems hungry soon after eating well, try offering play or a pacifier instead of going right to the bottle. If diarrhea persists or your baby seems ill, talk with her healthcare provider.

• **Gassiness.** Babies swallow a lot of air if they have to suck too hard or if the formula flows too fast, making them gulp. You can enlarge the hole in the nipple with a hot pin, or replace the nipple if the hole is too large. You also can try different nipple shapes. And as you feed your baby, be sure to hold the bottle at an angle to keep the nipple full of milk, not air.

• **Lactose intolerance.** Some babies inherit an inability to digest lactose, the main sugar in cow's-milk formulas. The symptoms are unusual gassiness, bloating of the intestines, diarrhea, and poor weight gain. A simple test done on a bowel movement can confirm this diagnosis. A soy-based or other lactose-free formula is an easy solution to alleviate this problem.

• **True food allergy.** About 1 in 20 infants has a true allergy to the protein in cow's milk—a very different problem from simple lactose intolerance. True milk allergy can cause bloody diarrhea, vomiting, irritability, rash, runny nose, wheezing, and other alarming symptoms. About a third of these babies are also allergic to soy protein. The usual treatment is to use an elemental formula that does not have either cow or soy proteins in it.

• **Attachment to the bottle.** It's not that uncommon for an older baby or toddler to get very attached to her bottle, but this can be a problem. Babies who become attached to their bottles and want to carry them around often develop severe dental cavities (or caries) because their teeth are bathed in sugar-containing formula for much of the day. Once your baby is finished drinking, it's a good idea to take the bottle away. Help her find another toy to carry around.

• **Sleeping with a bottle.** Babies who fall asleep with their bottles are also at risk for bad cavities, for the same reason. Putting water in the bedtime bottle avoids this particular problem. But any time a baby drinks a bottle lying flat on her back, fluid can run up the tube that connects the mouth to the ear, increasing the risk of ear infections. A good rule of thumb is no bottles in the crib.

Changing from formula to milk

Children should continue to drink commercially made infant formula until a year of age. After a year, babies can safely drink cow's milk. It's best to use whole milk up until age two years, because it provides the fat that toddlers need for healthy brain growth. After age two, children who get used to reduced-fat (1 or 2 percent or skim) milk are likely to have fewer problems with cholesterol-related heart disease when they are older.

Cow's milk is not, however, a dietary necessity. A few respected physicians (including Dr. Benjamin Spock in his lifetime) believe that cow's milk poses health risks at any age. For example, there is some evidence that eating dairy products increases the risk that a child will develop diabetes. It *is* possible to get adequate nutrition without any dairy at all, but you need to be well

---

CLASSIC SPOCK

"It has been discovered that babies enjoy just as much and do just as well on formula that is warmed, at room temperature, or right out of the refrigerator, as long as it comes at the same temperature each feeding."

— Dr. Benjamin Spock, *Baby and Child Care*

---

informed to do it. There is some information in Dr. Spock's *Baby and Child Care* if you're interested.

Weaning from the bottle

Most children can drink from a cup with assistance by the time they can hold their head steady while sitting—about six months. By nine months, many can handle a sippy cup (a cup with a lid containing a spout) on their own, and start using a small, regular cup around 12 to 15 months. If your baby has not become attached to her bottle as a comfort object, it shouldn't be hard to wean to a cup. While there is no benefit to weaning early, waiting too long just tends to make the process more difficult. A good plan is to start when your baby is six to nine months and gradually increase the frequency of drinking from a cup as your child gets better and better at it. At some point, you and your child can agree that the bottles aren't really getting used much, and it's time to give them to a baby who needs them.

It's not uncommon, though, for toddlers to get locked into battles with their parents over the bottle. The child wants to keep it; the parents want her to give it up. The parents plead or try to make deals; the toddler holds out. The parents take the bottles; the toddler has a tantrum and refuses the cup. Eventually, the parents give in. Everyone feels angry.

If you find yourself in this situation, there are a couple of ways you can go. One is simply to make the bottles disappear. You are sure to face a tantrum, or a string of tantrums spread out over a few days, but in the end your toddler will accept fluids from a cup and stop yearning for the bottle.

A less drastic approach is to insist that the bottle is for meals only, not for carrying around during the day or sleeping with at night. Once that's been established, you can gradually replace the bottle with a cup, one meal at a time. Another technique is to water down the milk in the bottle, adding a little more water each week until it is all water, while still serving milk in a cup. Usually before getting to this point, toddlers decide that the stuff from the cup (undiluted milk) tastes better.

Solid Foods

Once your baby starts taking solid foods, you both have many new choices. You must decide what foods to start with, how much to give, and how to set limits while still making eating fun. And your child must decide which foods to accept, how much to take, and how to have fun without getting you too upset!

A young baby even has to figure out the mechanics of eating solids: holding the food in his mouth and getting it down the right tube. He needs to be exposed to a wide variety of foods—usually cereals, vegetables, fruits, and meats, in more or less that order—with enough time in between new foods so that you can tell if he is going to show an early allergic reaction. Thankfully, your child usually participates willingly in these experiments in dining.

119

Around nine months of age, your baby has developed a will of his own—and a sense of humor—that presents new feeding challenges. Before, the cereal just dribbled out of his mouth because he lacked the proper coordination. Now he spits it out deliberately and laughs. Using his new, refined fine-motor skills, he accurately picks up individual peas and plays with them.

THE CASE FOR FLUORIDE

Fluoride is important for building healthy teeth that resist cavities. Up to age six months, babies don't need extra fluoride because their teeth haven't really developed. After six months, most bottle-fed babies get all the fluoride they need from the tap water used to mix their formula or cereal; breastfeeding moms, if they drink fluoridated tap water, pass on the fluoride to their babies. If you give your baby only pre-mixed formula or use only bottled water or non-fluoridated well water, you should give her fluoride supplements, as prescribed by her doctor. The usual dose is .25 mg per day. More is not better, however! Too much fluoride results in weak teeth with white spots, a condition called fluorosis.

Note: Check with your child's dentist or your local water or health department to see if your tap water is fluoridated.

If you try to feed him, he tries to grab the spoon because he wants to be in charge.

A toddler has definite likes and dislikes, and these change every day. So does his overall hunger, depending on how active he is and whether or not he is going through a growth spurt that week. Feeding him without engaging in useless power struggles takes a good deal of patience and creativity. By the time he goes off to preschool, however, he will have gained a great many eating skills, including the ability to be polite— well, at least in a preschooler kind of way.

How eating develops

Like other behaviors, eating solid food is a matter of physical maturation and practice. Here are some of the steps in this process:

• **Posture and reflexes.** To eat from a spoon, babies need to be able to sit in a chair comfortably and hold their heads steady for several minutes. They need to anticipate the coming spoon, open their mouths, and then close their lips tightly to keep the food in. They also have a little "unlearning" to do. Newborns are born with a strong sucking reflex that helps them nurse effectively. They suck on whatever goes into their mouths. This reflex needs to weaken—and usually does by four months of age—before babies can begin to use their mouths to eat solid foods.

• **Tongue coordination.** Babies have to teach their tongues some new tricks. For solid foods, the tongue

PARENT TO PARENT
*"We came to the conclusion
that our baby didn't know how to eat.
Seriously! It wasn't that she wasn't
interested in the foods, it was that
she didn't know that there is a certain
flow to how we eat. Open mouth,
spoon in, shut mouth around spoon,
allow spoon to depart, keep food
in mouth, swish (optional), swallow.
Repeat until full."*

— **danzam,** AS POSTED ON DRSPOCK.COM

first pushes the food sideways toward the gums or teeth, and then moves the softened food toward the back of the mouth. When there's a lot of food in the mouth, the tongue has to separate off a lump that is small enough to be swallowed, move that lump to the back, but hold the rest of the food forward.

• **The challenge of choking.** The opening to the trachea, or windpipe, lies just behind the tongue in the back of the mouth. The opening to the esophagus, the tube that food has to pass through on its way to the stomach, lies behind the trachea. Food has to move past the trachea in order to get into the esophagus, and this arrangement is really asking for trouble. Everyone has experienced food going down the "wrong tube"; it happens even to experienced eaters. For a baby, getting the food into the right tube can be a real challenge.

In order to help food pass by safely, the opening to the trachea has a partial covering. As the tongue pushes the food back and to the side, the tracheal covering protects the windpipe, and the esophagus opens to receive the small bit of food.

• **Learning takes time.** When broken down into steps like these, eating seems like a complex process, and, indeed, it takes time for babies to put all of these skills together. At first, many push the food out of their mouths with their tongues—a process known as the expulsion reflex. Tongue-thrusting works well when nursing because it helps strip the milk from the nipple, but it has to be unlearned for eating solid foods.

The sensation of having solid food in the mouth is strange at first, and some babies find it unpleasant. Early choking experiences can make babies tense when faced with a spoonful of food, and the tension makes the process of opening and accepting the food more difficult.

Practical tips

• **Wait until your baby can sit comfortably in an infant seat.** This is a developmental clue that your baby is ready to start solids.

• **Start with a very small amount on a small spoon, touched to your baby's lips.** Even after she gets used to the spoon and begins to willingly open up for it, still give her a very small amount for a while—no bigger than the size of a small lima bean.

• **Don't worry about food that slips out between her lips.** If your baby pushes the food out, don't automatically assume that she isn't interested. However, if she repeatedly pushes the food out, stop for now, and try again next meal. If she still continues to push the food out, wait a week before trying again.

• **If your baby begins to choke or sputter, slow down a bit.** There's no rush.

• **Expect a mess.** Feed your infant in a room with a floor that's easy to clean, or put a plastic tablecloth or spill mat (available at many baby stores) under her highchair.

• **If you feel that your baby is not making progress after a month, talk with her healthcare provider.** Various professionals, including speech therapists, occupational therapists, and physical therapists, can help babies who have problems learning to handle solid foods. After 9 or 10 months, infants who have not gotten comfortable with solid foods may have a harder time learning, so it is best not to wait too long.

What foods to give, and when

The traditional first food for a four- to six-month-old baby is iron-fortified rice cereal made especially for babies. It's nicely bland (although to a baby who has had only formula or breast milk, it may seem quite exotic!) and you can control the consistency. A moderately thin texture is good to start with, but not so runny that it simply pours down.

Start with just a small teaspoon, and gradually build up the amount, following your child's lead. You can add a different cereal every week or two. If you are concerned about allergies, you might want to hold off on introducing wheat for a while, since wheat allergies are fairly common. Using single-ingredient foods, rather than mixed ones, allows you to know what your child is reacting to if he develops a rash, diarrhea, or other allergic symptoms.

Once your infant gets the hang of some baby cereals, switch to a vegetable or a fruit. Babies who get used to the very sweet taste of fruits may balk at vegetables, so you may want to start with the vegetables and add the fruits later. You also can add juices, such as pear or apricot, in small quantities.

Foods that are good for beginning eaters

Whether you prepare your own or select from the wide array of commercial baby products, many foods are appropriate for beginning eaters, including:

• **Baby cereals:** rice, oats, corn, barley. Save wheat cereal for last.

• **Vegetables:** peas, beans, carrots, squash, sweet potatoes, beets. Save broccoli, onions, and cabbage for later; they are often strong tasting and can cause gas.

125

• **Fruits:** mashed bananas, stewed apples, pears, peaches, prunes, plums, apricots. The last five tend to act as mild laxatives, but most babies eat them without a problem.

• **Meats:** any soft, stewed meat is fine. Cut or grind the meat so that it isn't stringy. If you use very little salt, babies are less likely to develop a taste for salty foods, which later may contribute to high blood pressure. Another good source of protein is beans, boiled and mashed. There is a very wide variety to choose from. Current nutritional guidelines for adults recommend eating meat in small quantities, rather than having it be the centerpiece of the meal. It's probably a good idea for children to get used to this style of eating when they are quite young.

Foods to avoid for now
As mentioned above, it's best to avoid common causes of food allergies until your baby is at least one year old, particularly if your family has a history of hay fever, asthma, eczema, or other allergic problems. Foods to avoid include:

- Egg whites
- Peanuts and peanut butter
- Nuts and foods containing nuts
- Fish
- Shellfish
- Wheat

Up until a year of age, babies should not be given honey or corn syrup. Both of these can contain botulism spores,

SOLID FOODS B T

which are harmless to toddlers and older children but can make babies quite ill. There is also no reason to give babies those jarred "desserts" made with a lot of sugar. It only encourages them to develop a sweet tooth. It's better if babies come to see fruits as their sweets.

The battle of the spoons
If your eight- or nine-month-old baby reaches for the spoon when it's inches from his mouth and turns his head away, he may be full. More likely, though, he just wants to be in charge of the spoon. If you avoid his hand and trick him into opening his mouth, chances are that he will spit the food out and begin to fuss.

The solution is not to devise ever more creative ways to trick your baby (the old "Here's the airplane, open the hangar door wide" routine never fooled any baby, although plenty of them play along because it's a good game). What works better is to compromise. If you give your baby a spoon of his own, he can work at getting bits of food into his mouth while you "help out" with another spoon (and do the bulk of the feeding in the process).

Why toddlers seem to stop eating
Around age one, many toddlers seem to lose interest in food. Their eating slows down, and this decrease in appetite can be alarming to parents. But it's perfectly natural—toddlers eat less because they are no longer growing as quickly as they did as babies. A toddler who continued to gain weight as quickly as she did during the first months of life would quickly become obese.

Q: My son has been evaluated by our doctor and a nutritionist as having "texture aversion" and has not learned to chew and swallow well. He is otherwise active and healthy. Could you give me more information on this distressing problem, which I've learned is fairly common?

A: You're right, it's not uncommon for a young child to dislike the texture of certain foods because they are too crispy, mushy, or slimy. Many children have a mild aversion to a particular texture, but, with a little experimenting, their parents readily find a variety of other foods that they like very much. But other children are so oversensitive to texture that coming up with foods they will accept can be quite a challenge. Even though we don't know what causes this problem in the first place, we can still help children get over it. Your pediatrician and nutritionist can help you gradually expand your child's eating horizons while maintaining a healthy diet. Don't be surprised if your pediatrician also calls in other specialists. Often, occupational and speech therapists, who understand about mouth and tongue movements, are adept at teaching children to accept new textures in their mouths, as well as how to coordinate chewing and swallowing in a way that feels more comfortable to them.

How can you tell if your toddler is getting enough? First, she should have plenty of energy and curiosity. Poor concentration or a somber mood can be signs that a child is not taking in enough calories. Most important, your child's weight should continue to rise, following her established growth curve, as described at the beginning of this chapter. As long as your child is growing along her curve, you don't need to worry that she is getting too little food.

Pushing your child to eat more when she is not hungry is only likely to backfire. In response to a parent's pushing, a strong-willed toddler may refuse to eat, not because she is full, but simply in order to exert control. Being in charge is so important to some toddlers that they will actually go hungry if they feel that their parents are trying to force them to eat!

What can you do to help your toddler eat enough, without getting into a "food fight"?

• **Put small portions on her plate.** This way, she can ask for more (and thus be in charge).

• **Limit milk and juice intake.** Toddlers don't need any more than about 16 ounces of milk a day, and 6 to 8 ounces of juice at the most. Any more than that is likely to blunt their hunger for real food.

• **Cut down on distractions, such as television, during mealtimes.** Use a highchair to give your toddler a feeling of being contained at mealtimes. Sitting in the chair is a cue that it's time to eat.

• **Give your toddler mild approval when she eats.** For example, simply smile and say something pleasant.

• **If she pauses in eating, give her a few minutes to get hungry again.** But do not disapprove when she stops, and do not try to get her to eat more by playing games.

• **If your child plays with her food a little, ignore it.** Telling her to stop is only likely to encourage her to play more; after all, it's great fun to get Mom's or Dad's attention! But if she starts playing with the food in earnest, or tries to get down from the highchair, end the meal. If she doesn't eat enough at one meal, she'll be hungrier at the next one.

• **Give your child a variety of foods, not just the ones that are her current favorites.** It's OK to encourage a child to taste new foods, or retry foods she hasn't much cared for in the past, but don't insist that she eat a lot of such food. Instead, let her fill up on the nutritious foods she prefers.

• **If you are concerned that your toddler may not be eating enough, arrange a visit with her doctor.** He'll weigh her and talk to you about ways to make sure that she gets adequate nutrition.

Broadening your toddler's food horizons

Why are so many toddlers so picky about what they'll eat? Of course, food probably isn't the only thing that your toddler is picky about. Chances are, he'll only want a certain pair of pajamas day after day, a certain toy to play with, or a certain chair to sit in. Toddlers are picky, in part, because they are just discovering how to form opinions and make independent choices about all sorts of things.

Toddlers can afford to be picky about food because they aren't growing as fast as they did when they were babies, so they aren't as hungry all the time. They can hold out for what they want. What can you do when this newly empowered young person flat-out refuses to eat anything except peanut butter and jelly?

As a parent, the last thing you want to do is get into a struggle over food with your toddler. This is a fight you can't win. You can't safely force a child to swallow food

Classic Spock
"Don't urge babies to take more than they are eager for. Let them go on enjoying their meals, feeling that you are their friend. This is one of the principal ways in which their self-confidence, their joy in life, and their love of people will be firmly established during the first year."

— Dr. Benjamin Spock, *Baby and Child Care*

(although physical force does sometimes come into play with medications). And bribery—"you can only have dessert after you finish your peas"—tends to backfire in the long run. Your child might eat the peas, but afterward he is even more convinced than ever that he hates peas! Here are some more effective strategies:

• **Put a small portion of any new food you want your child to take on his plate several meals in a row.** Once he has seen it a few times, it won't be new (and therefore suspect) anymore, and he'll be more likely to be adventuresome and taste it.

• **Don't make a big fuss when your child refuses a new food—or when he takes it.** Let eating be its own reward.

• **Be a good role model.** Let your child see you eating and enjoying a variety of healthy foods.

• **If your child asks for a particular, nutritious food several days in a row, go ahead and give it to him.** Chances are good that he'll tire of it and soon move on to another favorite. If your child eats a reasonable mix of foods over the course of a week, that's fine, even if he only eats one kind of food each day.

• **It's also OK to set limits on food choice.** Your child has a right to refuse to eat any particular food on any particular day. But he does not have the right to demand that you cook something special for him. If your menu includes at least one or two items that are reasonably child-friendly and your toddler decides to sit out a particular meal, that's his business.

• **Be creative.** If your child refuses a particular food (broccoli, say), try to substitute another food with similar qualities (kale, for example, or spinach).

• **If your toddler refuses a whole food group, such as all green vegetables, you can substitute foods from other groups.** For example, apples supply fiber, squashes supply vitamins, and kidney beans and other legumes supply iron and protein. Many children refuse all vegetables except one—either corn or peas, for example. It's fine to give them that one vegetable over and over, while also putting small amounts of other vegetables on the plate.

• **Some children are sensitive to particular textures.** They may refuse any foods that are crunchy or any that are "slimy." Once you know this, you can use your creativity to make more foods acceptable. For example, creamed corn is on the slimy side, but frozen corn (which is a fine finger food for a two-year-old) is crunchy.

• **A chewable children's multivitamin is a good way to take some of the pressure off eating.** Ideally, children will get all their vitamins and minerals from the food they eat. But it doesn't always work out that way. If you give your child a multivitamin, at least you can feel assured that she is getting most or all of what she needs. You can then relax a bit about the vegetables.

Why babies make messes

Young babies and toddlers make a mess when they eat. It's not just that their aim is bad and their hands unsteady. They make messes on purpose. One messy behavior that drives a lot of parents mad is called casting; deliberately tossing a piece of food off the highchair, waiting for you to pick it up, then laughing and tossing the same food again. This may seem like a great game, but your child is actually doing a scientific experiment, finding out that, yes, food always drops down, never up. And he also discovers that if the food disappears from view, it can reappear.

Although casting is often trying for parents, your baby also sees it as a fun way to engage socially. For a young child, there are few things more amusing than getting someone to respond in a predictable way. It gives him a delightful sense of being in control. Other ways of playing with food—smearing it on the highchair tray, for instance—can be seen as a baby's experimenting with colors and textures, or just expressing himself creatively in his chosen medium: dinner.

Recognizing these positive aspects of mess-making does not mean that you have to put up with it beyond a certain point. It's fine to simply end the meal and suggest another activity.

Mealtimes will become more pleasant, and your child will be able to explore new foods at her own pace.

• **Try to avoid making sweets a reward** for "good" eating. Children who come to prize sugary foods when they are young are more apt to indulge frequently when they are older and have more access to the foods they like best.

Feeding Supplies

Walk into any baby store and you're bound to be amazed by the variety of feeding supplies on the market. Some are practical and helpful, some are downright ingenious, and some, frankly, are a bit silly. This section is designed to help you navigate the crowded aisles and find the products that will really be of use to you.

BREASTFEEDING SUPPLIES

For an activity that's 100 percent natural and older than *Homo sapiens*, breastfeeding requires an awful lot of supplies! Here are some popular ones to consider:

• **Clothing.** During your pregnancy, you'll have stocked up on supportive bras to accommodate your new bustline. Add to those several nursing bras with flaps that lower, giving your infant easier access. Nicely designed shirts with hidden flap openings make it easier to nurse in public without embarrassment, and nursing nightgowns also come in handy for late-night feedings. Maternity shops and many department stores carry a large selection of both. Although it might be a little bit of overkill, some manufacturers also make special nursing shawls and cover-ups to allow a mom a bit more modesty while breastfeeding in public.

• **Breast pump.** One piece of equipment that few nursing mothers can live without is a good, hospital-quality, electric breast pump, especially if they're continuing to breastfeed while working outside the home. With an efficient pump, you can empty your breasts in about 10 minutes, keeping your milk supply up and preventing painful engorgement. You can buy hand-operated and battery-operated pumps for less, but they take much, much longer, even if your hand muscles don't give out first. A high-quality electric pump with a "double-barreled" collecting system allows you to empty both breasts simultaneously. It is simply the fastest way of pumping, and therefore the only way for many busy women. The catch is, these machines are quite expensive, usually running $300 to $500 or more. Many hospitals and hospital-supply stores rent them for reasonable rates, however, and some health insurance plans cover the expense.

• **Nursing pads.** These soft, round pads fit into bras to help absorb any leakage and prevent chafing. Usually made of cotton, they are available in both washable and disposable models.

Breastfeeding supplies checklist

☐ Nursing shirts

☐ Nursing nightgowns

☐ Nursing bras

☐ Nursing shawls or cover-ups

☐ Burp cloths (cloth diapers draped over your shoulder work well for this purpose, too)

☐ Nursing pads

☐ Nipple shields

☐ Breast pump

☐ Breast shields

☐ Containers and bottles for storing expressed breast milk

☐ Bottle and nipple brushes

☐ Nursing pillow

☐ Lanolin or glycerin gel pads

☐ Rocking chair

☐ Nursing footrest

• **Lanolin and gel pads.** A tube of pure lanolin or a set of glycerin gel pads can soothe sore nipples and help them heal faster.

• **Breast and nipple shields.** Breast shields are dome-shaped plastic shells that fit over breasts to provide greater comfort while pumping. Nipple shields are thin plastic shells with a hole in the middle that fit into bras. They protect delicate or sore nipples from rubbing against clothing and provide greater air circulation to help the nipples stay dry. Some experts—and moms—swear by them; others don't think they're necessary. Certain nipple shields are specifically designed to draw out flat or inverted nipples, making it easier for a baby to latch on.

• **Nursing pillow.** To ease the strain on your back and arms, a pillow that supports your baby while nursing is a helpful item. You can use any small, firm pillow, but you might find a nursing pillow, which is made to fit the contours of your lap and elevate your baby to just the right height, even more comfortable for this purpose. They are available in baby-supply stores, or you can find them online.

• **Rocking chair.** This popular nursery staple provides a convenient and cozy breastfeeding perch. Look for one with good back support and arms positioned at the right height for you. Seat cushions will make the chair even more comfortable—and a little footrest can do wonders for tired legs.

BOTTLE-FEEDING SUPPLIES

There are very few supplies that you need for bottle-feeding that aren't completely self-evident (that is, bottles and nipples). You can opt for reusable bottles, which must be cleaned thoroughly after each feeding, or disposable bottles, which use collapsible, throwaway plastic liners. A few additional items to consider include:

• **Bottle brushes.** These should be solely dedicated to cleaning your baby's bottles. You should have one for the bottles and a smaller one for scrubbing out the nipples.

• **A selection of nipples.** Make sure they have different shapes and hole sizes. None is superior to the others (claims of nipples' being "orthodontically correct" are just advertising), but as your baby grows, he might prefer one type over another.

• **An insulated tote bag.** This makes it easier to keep prepared formula chilled when you are on the road.

• **A dishwasher rack for nipples and bottle collars.** Not strictly necessary, of course, but this little cage-like device helps keep nipples and bottle collars in place in the top rack of the dishwasher.

• **An electric or battery-powered bottle warmer.** When you're at home, this is really an unnecessary luxury, as a pan of warm water does just as well. (Remember that microwaves can produce hot spots within a bottle of

BOTTLE-FEEDING SUPPLIES CHECKLIST

☐ A supply of cow's-milk or soy formula

☐ Plastic or disposable bottles

☐ Plastic liners for disposable bottles, if necessary

☐ An assortment of nipples

☐ Bottle brushes—a small, narrow one for cleaning out nipples and a larger one for washing out plastic bottles

☐ An insulated tote bag for carrying bottle-feeding supplies

☐ An electric or portable bottle warmer

☐ A dishwasher rack for nipples and collars

☐ Burp cloths

☐ Bibs (to help keep baby's clothes clean while feeding)

☐ A rocking chair

☐ A nursing footrest

☐ A nursing pillow (made for breastfeeding moms, but bottle-feeding parents get tired arms and backs, too)

milk that could scald your baby.) However, when you're on the road, a battery-powered bottle warmer, or one that plugs into your car's cigarette lighter, can come in handy if your baby doesn't like his milk chilled.

FEEDING SUPPLIES FOR THE OLDER BABY

Once your baby graduates to a cup or begins to eat solid foods, a whole new world of feeding supplies awaits you. Some of these items truly make life easier on you and your eager eater; others definitely fall into the nice-but-not-necessary category.

Highchairs
When you first start feeding your baby solid foods, it's fine to sit her up in an infant seat or hold her on your lap (be sure to put on a big apron first!). Once she starts moving around more on her own—usually by seven or eight months, if not before—you'll need a highchair. If you use the highchair for every meal, your baby will soon learn that sitting in this particular chair means it's time to eat. When babies and toddlers know what's expected of them, they are more likely to comply.

Highchair safety
Although extremely common and useful, highchairs can be dangerous. In fact, the U.S. Consumer Product Safety Commission (CPSC) reports that there are thousands of highchair injuries each year. Here is a summary of the CPSC safety recommendations.

- **Use restraining straps.** Always use all of the straps provided, especially the crotch strap. A baby who slides forward under the tray can end up hanging from his neck with his body dangling over the edge of the chair.

- **Use the locking device.** Be sure the locking device on a folding chair is set during use; otherwise, the chair could collapse.

- **Keep your child seated.** Never allow your child to stand up in his chair, or climb onto the chair without help.

- **Stay close.** You may need to step in quickly, especially if your toddler has shown that he can unbuckle the straps.

- **Position the chair properly.** Keep the chair far enough away from the table, counter, or wall so that your child can't push off with his hands or feet, and possibly tip himself over.

- **No climbing.** Don't let older children hang onto the highchair when your baby is in it—that, too, can cause it to tip over.

When buying or borrowing a highchair, look for the following key safety features (again from the CPSC):

- **A wide base.** This will help keep it from tipping.

- **A design that prevents the child from slipping out.** If the chair is equipped with restraining straps, you shouldn't be able to buckle the waist strap unless you also use the crotch strap. An alternate design is a chair with a post between the legs, which also prevents a child from slipping down and out. You'd be surprised how quickly this can happen.

• **Easy-to-use buckles.** You'll really appreciate this seemingly simple feature when you're trying to maneuver a squirming baby into a highchair.

Other things to look for in a highchair include a tray that is removable, easy to wash, and large enough so at least some of the food that spills off the plate stays on the tray. A padded seat is nice for comfort (although you might think that your baby has enough padding already!). A foldable seat is almost a must if the space in your kitchen is limited—just be sure to use the locking device properly.

Clip-on chairs

As an alternative to a highchair, some parents choose a chair that clips onto the edge of a table, allowing a baby to sit right up to the table. One drawback of these devices is that there is no tray to keep your baby's food all in more or less one place. Safety is another concern. All of the safety tips that apply to highchairs apply to clip-on chairs. In addition, be sure that your child can't dislodge the chair from the table, and that the table itself can't be knocked over if your child pushes on it with his feet. (Personally speaking, these chairs make me nervous.)

Booster seats

A safer and sturdier alternative to a clip-on chair (though probably still not as safe as a highchair), a booster seat can be used alone on the floor or strapped into place on a regular chair. Portable, fold-up models are available for babies on the go.

OTHER FEEDING SUPPLIES

In addition to a highchair, other helpful mealtime supplies include:

• **Kiddie spoons.** Any small spoon will do, of course, but there are lots of special spoons that can make feeding easier. Look for spoons that have a padded bowl, or that are made out of plastic. These are much less harsh on babies' gums and palates than metal spoons. Spoons with wide, short handles make it possible for infants and toddlers who are intent on self-feeding to actually succeed some of the time. Spoons that have the bowl set off at an angle can also make self-feeding a bit easier. Once your toddler has mastered the fine art of using a spoon, you might want to branch out into kiddie forks, with short handles and small, blunt tines.

• **Bibs.** There are many types available: cloth bibs, plastic bibs, bibs with crumb-catchers on the bottom, bibs that cover a baby's arms as well as his chest, bibs that tie, bibs that slip on over a baby's head, even fancy bibs adorned with satin and lace for dress-up occasions.

Most aren't very expensive, so you can experiment and see which ones work best for you.

• **Cups.** A tippy cup is weighted on the bottom and has a lid with a drinking spout. A sippy cup isn't weighted, but it, too, has a lid with a spout. Both help your toddler get used to drinking from a cup and cut down on spills.

FEEDING SUPPLIES CHECKLIST

☐ Bowls

☐ Partitioned plates

☐ Padded baby spoons

☐ Toddler-size spoons and forks

☐ Bibs

☐ Spill mat

☐ Highchair

☐ Booster or clip-on chair (better for occasional, rather than everyday, use)

☐ Tippy or sippy cups

☐ Food grinder

• **Bowls and plates.** Small bowls with suction-cup bottoms adhere firmly to a highchair tray or table, making for a more stable eating surface (and fewer bowls launched into space!). A partitioned plate, with separate areas for three or four different foods, can be a great help with toddlers who feel passionately that mashed potatoes must never, ever come in contact with applesauce.

• **Spill mats.** Positioned under a highchair or clip-on chair, these square, easily cleaned plastic mats can be your floor's best friend.

• **Food grinders.** These small manual devices let you convert regular food into baby food by chopping it up into little pieces. Of course, you also can use a blender or food processor instead.

CHAPTER 3

Comforting

*"At first, crying is a baby's only form of
communication with the outside, new world
and has many meanings, not just pain or sadness.
As she grows older, crying is much less of a problem
because you worry less, you know what to expect
from her at different times of the day, you are
able to distinguish between different cries, and
she has fewer reasons to cry."*

— Dr. Benjamin Spock, *Baby and Child Care*

Comforting is a basic need, like food and safety. Baby monkeys raised without maternal contact don't survive. Human babies raised in impersonal institutions, without loving relationships, grow up stunted, both physically and emotionally. And just as babies need comforting, parents have a need to give comfort. What is more fulfilling than to hold a crying baby and have her relax, quiet down, and snuggle in? And what is more demoralizing than picking up a crying baby and having her scream and arch away?

COMFORTING

Comforting is very much a here-and-now activity: The main goal is to help your child get through a particular rough moment, and move on. But there are long-term effects, too. Each time you comfort your baby, you learn more about her. You come to know what upsets her, and what she needs to feel better. At the same time, your child comes to know and trust you, and, in turn, learns how to be a comforting person herself. You can see this in the three-year-old who lovingly cradles her doll, saying, "Don't cry, baby." A young child who is well and wisely comforted also has a stock of inner reassurance to draw upon when faced with life's inevitable challenges later on.

Comforting a crying baby is a natural reaction, but it isn't always easy. Some babies get upset more often than others, and have a harder time calming down. And babies who have colic can cry for hours in spite of everything their parents try. As babies turn into toddlers, their needs for comforting change. They are better able to handle common physical stresses—hunger, for example—but face new emotional challenges such as being apart from their parents or dealing with imaginary monsters. These new upsets require different kinds of comforting.

Whether you're just learning to interpret your baby's different cries or dealing with a fretful toddler, the information in this chapter is designed to help you gain confidence and competence in soothing your child. I also hope, by giving you insights into your child's mind and emotional needs, that it will help you handle those times (that happen to us all!) when things don't go smoothly.

Comforting Basics

Your baby won't be shy about announcing when he needs to be comforted. Chances are, he'll ask for attention by crying loudly and lustily. A crying baby is hard to ignore. The wailing drives many adults, and especially parents, crazy. And, in a way, it should. Crying is one of the few ways that babies can let us know that they need our help. It's very likely that infant crying evolved because it is such a powerful way to get an adult's attention and protection. Both a baby's crying and a parent's need to respond seem to be driven by strong instincts. The fact that your baby's crying is so upsetting shows how very tightly you and he are bound together.

Every baby cries sometimes. Newborns usually cry very little in the first week or two of life, but then begin crying more and more. The greatest amount of crying, on average, occurs when babies are about six weeks old. At that age, a healthy baby may cry for three or more hours out of 24. After that, crying gradually tapers off, so that by three or four months, most babies are crying for a total of an hour or less a day.

Nobody really knows what causes this age-related peak in crying. One clue is that it seems to occur in many different cultures, all over the world. This suggests that there is a biological explanation. As I men-

KEY: Ⓝ =Newborn (0-2 mos.) Ⓑ =Baby (2 mos.-1 yr.) Ⓣ =Toddler (1-3 yrs.)

149

tioned in the chapter on sleep, most babies spend the first three months of life sorting out night and day and getting onto a reasonable sleep schedule. So perhaps all that crying has to do with the baby's sleep cycle's being out of sync, sort of like jet lag. Whatever the explanation, don't be surprised if you find your baby doing a lot of crying around one to two months of age, for no good reason that you can see.

Crying teaches babies—and parents—a lot

Crying is a baby's first experience with cause and effect. He learns to expect that his crying will cause a trusted grown-up to appear and make him feel better. Even a very young baby seems to develop this positive expectation, and it becomes a basic part of his relationship with his parents. The deep-seated belief that "Mommy and Daddy make things better and keep me safe" follows a child throughout life, and helps him handle the normal stresses of childhood, such as staying with a new babysitter or going off to school for the first time.

Of course, no parent is perfectly responsive, and, thankfully, you don't have to be. Sometimes you can respond immediately after your baby starts crying, but other times it takes you a while longer. These little delays are not a bad thing. Rather, they give your child the motive and the opportunity to begin to develop self-calming skills (as I described in the first chapter). It is only when parents regularly wait far too long or don't respond at all that a baby is likely to feel alone, helpless, and depressed.

Parents can learn from their babies' crying, as well. Through experience, you'll be able to distinguish different cries—for example, hunger versus tiredness versus boredom—and the responses that are most effective. In this way, you will come to feel more and more capable. Depending on your child, there are bound to be a few, or possibly many, instances when nothing stops the crying except the passage of time. From these miserable experiences you may learn that you have reserves of patience and nurturing that you never thought you had. These tough lessons are likely to come in handy

Parent to Parent

"I have a two-year-old boy and a one-year-old girl. My husband and I always made a point of being affectionate and encouraging with them. They are now affectionate with each other and genuinely care about each other's feelings. I think that the more loving and supportive we are when our children are young, the more secure and well rounded they will be as adults."

— **sister,** AS POSTED ON DRSPOCK.COM

STATES OF AROUSAL

State 1: Deep Sleep (very low arousal)
The baby may not respond to fairly loud noises and bright lights.

State 2: Light Sleep (low arousal)
The baby responds to noises or lights by moving or grimacing, or by waking up more.

State 3: Drowsy (moderately low arousal)
The baby is halfway between sleep and waking. A little stimulus is likely to wake him all the way.

State 4: Awake and Alert (moderate arousal)
The baby is interested in looking at things and listening, especially when his parents talk to him. His face shows happiness, interest, or surprise.

State 5: Fussy (mild overarousal)
The baby seems to be more tuned in to his own distress, and as a result is less responsive to what's going on around him.

State 6: Crying (overarousal)
In this state, the baby is almost completely focused on his discomfort. The sound of his own crying and the feeling of his own tensed muscles tend to keep him overaroused until he falls asleep, exhausted.

later, as you and your child face the challenges of middle childhood and adolescence.

Crying provides a clue to a baby's level of arousal

Another way to think of crying is that it occurs when babies are overly aroused. In clinical terms, "arousal" refers to a person's degree of alertness or responsiveness to stimulation. Dr. T. Berry Brazelton, the famous pediatrician, has explained how babies move from one state of arousal to another through the course of their day.

The connection between crying and arousal helps explain why some attempts at comforting work, while others don't. If a child is fussy (State 5), a parent's too vigorous attempts to calm her down—for example, singing, patting, and rocking all at once—may only add to the overarousal, pushing her into State 6. A child who is crying uncontrollably (State 6) may not respond to mild soothing attempts (a lullaby, for example) because she is too upset to pay attention to them; all of her attention is focused on internal feelings of discomfort and tension. Soothing that starts out by matching the intensity of the child's arousal—matching rocking to the rhythm of the baby's crying, for example—can sometimes capture the child's attention, after which you can gradually bring the level of arousal down.

Arousal also helps explain why some children with special needs are so difficult to comfort. For example, very premature infants are often hypersensitive to stimulation, so that they are easily overaroused. As a result, they jump from drowsy (State 3) right to fussy or screaming (States 5 and 6), without pausing at awake and alert

(State 4). They may defend themselves from being over-stimulated by closing their eyes and appearing to fall asleep. But if you turn down the lights and speak very quietly to them, they open their eyes and look around. If you try to make prolonged eye contact at the same time that you're talking, however, that might be too much stimulation. Watch your baby's cues closely—you'll get better and better at reading them.

Children learn self-soothing skills

The thought that you are solely responsible for your child's contentment can be a frightening responsibility, especially for a brand-new parent. And while it's true that young children rely on their parents to soothe them when they're upset, even from the beginning, babies also have surprising self-calming abilities. If you disturb a sleeping baby, he may stir, wriggle, somehow get a hand up to his mouth, suck three or four times, and settle back to sleep. In this sequence, he shows how he is able to handle unwanted stimulation without getting flustered.

Later, you might watch that baby as he "talks" with his mother. First, the infant babbles and the mom coos back. Then the baby gives a more excited little yelp, which his mom returns in kind. Back and forth they go, all the while getting more and more excited. Clearly, this game can't go on forever, and it doesn't. At a certain point, when the excitement reaches his limits of comfort, the baby breaks off. He turns away or looks down. His face falls. His mom, too, is quiet. Then, after a short rest, the game starts again.

This is another example of how babies soothe themselves, by backing off before they become over-stimulated. A less mature baby might not have put on the brakes as effectively, and instead burst into tears just as the game seemed to be at its peak. A less tuned-in mother might have kept on talking, even after her baby turned away. Overwhelmed now, the baby might have shown his stress by crying, shaking, or even throwing up. So you see how babies and their parents have to work as a team for soothing to be effective.

Eventually, of course, children learn how to calm themselves down without always needing help from their parents. But this process takes a long time. At two years of age, children are still easily swept up and away by strong emotions, positive and negative. At three, they may be able to handle minor frustrations, such as waiting to eat dinner, but lose it when confronted with a bigger challenge, such as watching a sibling get a present that they themselves want. By six, some children will have well-developed self-soothing abilities, but others will need many more years to mature. Helping your child develop his self-soothing ability is really a long-term project.

Sometimes comfort objects help

As they mature, many young children learn to rely on a comfort object to keep themselves calm or to settle down to sleep. Early on, babies often seem to enjoy pet-ting a soft cloth or running the fringe through their fingers, a habit known as silking. Around 18 months, when separations from parents are especially hard for many toddlers, a special blanket and beloved teddy bear can help. Parents sometimes worry that their children will become dependent on their blankies, but this rarely is a problem. Children generally use these objects until they don't need them anymore, and then give them up.

There are a few precautions to keep in mind, however: Up until 12 months of age, you should keep the crib free of loose blankets, fluffy pillows and comforters, and stuffed toys, in keeping with the standard precautions to prevent SIDS (see page 6). For toddlers, large stuffed animals aren't ideal comfort objects, since they are hard to carry around and children sometimes use them to stand on while climbing out of their cribs. Smaller stuffed animals are fine for toddlers, as long as the toys meet safety standards, such as not having any glued- or sewn-on parts like eyes and noses that could break off and pose a choking hazard. Baby bottles don't make good comfort objects, because going to sleep with a milk or juice bottle often results in severe tooth decay and increases the risk of ear infections.

Comforting Issues at Different Ages

To brand-new parents, a baby's cries all sound alike. When she starts wailing, they have no idea if their baby is hungry, tired, hurt, frightened, upset, or in need of a diaper change. They often can't tell how urgent the cry is—if they need to rush to her side immediately to rescue her from a poking safety pin, or if she's simply fussy and might calm down on her own if they wait a minute or two. But, over time, they are sure to learn a new language: the distinct sounds and meanings of their baby's different cries.

NEWBORNS AND BABIES

As a new parent, your first attempts are sure to rely on trial and error. You talk to your baby, hold her, and check her diaper. If that doesn't work, you offer a bottle or breast, or maybe try one of the other comforting techniques I describe later. Over time, you come to know your baby better, and can begin to make more sense of her cries. You learn to tell a hunger cry from one that means

PARENT TO PARENT
"If your child has a 'lovey' blankie or bear, try leaving it with him if he's having a hard time handling separations from you. Also, before you go, always tell him that you will be back to get him. Small as he is, he will learn to trust you because you DO come back. Then leave quickly after goodbyes . . . no use dragging out the sad time."

— **jeremysmom,** AS POSTED ON DRSPOCK.COM

"I'm wet" or "Pick me up!" Because you are tuned in to your baby's feelings and reactions, her cries are transformed. They aren't just irritating noise. They become communication, and you become fluent in her language.

Of course, your baby contributes to this process, too. Babies who give clear cues about what the matter is—crying at particular times in a particular way to indicate hunger, for example—help parents respond effectively. Just as with sleeping and eating (see Chapters 1 and 2), soothing requires a partnership between baby and parent. That means that when it works well, you deserve some credit, but so does your baby. And if soothing is not working, you can't simply blame yourself. As I discussed earlier, some babies are by their very nature more difficult to soothe than others.

Can you spoil a baby?

Some parents worry that if they pick up their infants too much or don't give them a chance to cry, they will "spoil" the infants. Actually, this is a sensible worry, since it is certainly possible to spoil an older child by always giving him what he wants immediately. One of the most important lessons a child can learn is to be able to wait for something he wants—even be denied it once in a while.

However, it's different with babies. It is *not* possible to spoil an infant. In fact, when parents respond quickly to their babies' crying, on the whole the babies are less likely to cry a lot when they are older, and more likely to be able to soothe themselves. (By responding to a baby's cry, I mean changing a diaper, giving a breast or bottle, holding and rocking, or doing something else to calm the baby down.)

Comforting an upset baby does not spoil him, but just the opposite. If this conclusion seems illogical to you, consider the following:

• **A three-month-old does not have the ability to use imagination or language to help with waiting.** For a baby, waiting really means simply enduring the discomfort of wetness or hunger that seems to last forever (since he cannot imagine the future).

• **Babies who are made to wait too much either become very fussy and impossible to satisfy, or they become very quiet.** In effect, they give up trusting that, in time, their needs will be met. When they grow older, these misgivings actually make it harder for them to wait for what they want.

• **Even the most caring and dedicated parent can't respond instantly to a baby's needs.** You have other things to do, and you can't always be right by his side. So every baby gets some experience with waiting, in small doses. Babies learn a lot from these little waiting periods. As they wait, they become distressed. But pretty soon, their mother, father, or caregiver shows up and makes everything better. In this way, the baby comes to rely on certain people, and to trust them to care for him. If a baby never had to wait at all, he would never experience the feeling of wonderful relief when a loved adult comes into view.

• **There are also times when parents are wise not to rush in right away to soothe an upset baby.** For example, when a four-month-old wakes in the night and fusses a bit, it's fine to give him a few moments to settle himself back to sleep. But if the baby can't settle, or begins to cry more, then it makes sense to comfort him before he gets too worked up (see Chapter 1).

• **Comforting a crying baby is a natural reaction.** Most mothers I talk with say that they want to comfort their crying babies, even if they believe that doing so will somehow spoil the infants. In fact, they have to use all of their willpower to stop themselves from picking up their babies. I try to encourage these moms to trust their mothering instincts, and in particular, the very strong instinct to comfort a crying baby.

Comforting a fearful baby

In infants, fear is an instinct. Loud noises, sudden movements, and unfamiliar people all trigger fearful crying. Back when we lived in caves (or maybe trees), the infants who had the strongest fear response were the ones who survived. That may explain why infant fearfulness is still with us, even though the threat of being eaten by wild beasts has pretty much disappeared.

In the beginning, soothing infant fears is mainly about physical contact. If you want to comfort a fearful baby, hold her. By eight or nine months, most infants learn to pay attention to the expressions on their parents' faces. If a parent looks calm and unthreatened, the baby relaxes, too. Babies also respond to a reassuring tone of voice, even if they don't understand the words.

Fear of strangers is a natural reaction

When I walk into the exam room to see a four-month-old, I expect to find a bright, curious little person who greets me without any fear. A few months later, that same child clutches his mother's neck in terror and wails as I approach. What happened? Normal development, that's what! Around six to nine months of age, babies discover that the world is made up of two kinds of people: those they know and strangers.

The first sign of stranger awareness is when a baby looks first at the new person, then back at his parent's face. If the parent is smiling, the baby often smiles, too; if the parent looks anxious or angry, the baby reacts with fear. Whether he screams in terror or just stares at the stranger with a worried look on his face is the result of the baby's innate temperament. Some babies are naturally more fearful, and some express their emotions more forcefully than others. The timing also varies from child to child. For many, the height of stranger anxiety is around 15 to 24 months, a time when many children go through an intense clingy phase.

When a seven-month-old reacts with fear, a parent usually can calm the baby by holding him close and speaking soothingly to him. A wise stranger knows to approach slowly, to give the baby time to get used to him. When an older child reacts with fear, parents sometimes are less sure how to respond. They are apt to feel that they need to do something to make their

CLASSIC SPOCK
"Spoiling doesn't come from being good to a baby in a sensible way, and it doesn't come all of a sudden. Spoiling comes on gradually when parents are too afraid to use their common sense, or when they really want to be slaves and encourage their babies to become slave drivers."

— Dr. Benjamin Spock, *Baby and Child Care*

children quiet down right away. Some well-meaning parents tease their children for being "scaredy cats," or actually get angry at them for feeling frightened. In the long run, neither of these approaches helps a child grow up confident and unafraid.

Most often, when an older child is very uncomfortable around strangers, the culprit is temperament. About one in seven children has a temperamental trait called "slow to warm up." Their first response to a social situation is to try to disappear into a corner. But given time, they get more comfortable and can join the party. Some people call this shyness, although I think that has a negative connotation.

The slow-to-warm-up trait is inherited. It is not the result of bad parenting, nor can even the most skillful parents change it. The best you can do is to accept your child for who he is. To the pleasant stranger (or the possibly offended relative), you can simply explain that your child takes a while to warm up to new people. You might say, "He'll feel more comfortable saying hello in a few minutes." At the same time, your words reassure your child that the person really is nice and that he'll feel better about things soon. A gentle hand on your child's shoulder lets him know you're there, but doesn't encourage him to be babyish or dependent. You're saying, in effect, "I expect you to be sociable, when you're ready." In the end, what your child takes away from the situation is your calm, reassuring presence and the feeling of being accepted by you—a powerful memory he can turn to in the future whenever a situation makes him feel anxious.

Thumb-sucking and pacifiers have a calming effect

Even before they are born, some babies begin to suck. We knew this before ultrasound gave us photographic proof because many newborns arrive in the world with a thickened patch of skin on their hands or the side of one arm. Two-week-old babies often manage to get a hand to their mouths and suck briefly, but their uncoordinated movements make it hard for them to keep the hand there for long. By about four months, most babies are able to suck on their fingers, thumbs, or hands at will.

Sucking serves two functions. It's how infants take in nutrients, of course, and it is also a powerful means of self-calming. Sucking sets off reflexes that cause the heart to slow and the muscles to relax. These are the opposite of the so-called fight-or-flight responses caused by stress.

Parents are often concerned when they notice their young babies beginning to suck their thumbs. I try to convince them that it is actually a good thing. A baby who can suck her thumb has a built-in way of calming herself that never gets lost. Nearly all babies suck their thumbs at some point, but only a very few keep on past age three or four years, at least in public. In most cases, thumb-sucking is something children use when they need it, and stop after they develop other ways of calming themselves down.

Thumb-sucking rarely causes medical problems, although children who live in older houses with peeling paint run an increased risk of lead poisoning, particularly if they regularly suck their thumbs. The solution, however, is to clean up the environment, not to try to change the baby's behavior. Children who suck their thumbs vigorously many hours a day often develop sucking calluses or thumbs that bend back too far. A child who continues to suck her thumb past around six years of age, when the adult teeth begin to come in, may develop an overbite or other orthodontic problems. Doctors rarely worry about thumb-sucking under age four.

Everything I've said about thumb-sucking applies to pacifiers, too. Of course, pacifiers aren't attached the way thumbs are, so they can fall out of the crib or end up under the cushions of the couch. You have to rinse them off frequently, or they tend to gather dust. They also can sometimes harbor *Candida*, the fungus that causes thrush (white patches on the inside of a baby's cheeks that look like milk but don't wipe off and often hurt). Even though some pacifiers bill themselves as "orthodontically correct," I don't think that there is any real difference between brands, although a baby might have a preference for a particular shape.

There are also a few important safety issues to keep in mind: (1) Pacifiers should not be attached to a baby's clothing using a ribbon or cord that could strangle the baby. (2) It is not safe to use the nipple from a baby's bottle as a pacifier. The nipple can come apart, and the baby can choke on the pieces. (3) Parents sometimes stuff paper or other objects into the nipple to keep the baby from sucking in air. But these things often fall out, and become choking hazards as well.

Practical tips

• **When it comes to comforting a crying baby, try the basics first.** Check his diaper, consider whether it's time for a feeding, see if a few minutes of being held in your arms calms your baby down.

• **Breastfeeding may help.** Even if a baby isn't that hungry, nursing has a powerful calming effect. In one study, newborn babies were observed while they had their heels pricked for the routine filter-paper screening blood tests. Babies who were nursing during the heel-prick barely cried, compared with other, non-feeding babies who (as one would expect) wailed loudly. It's not clear whether or not bottle-feeding has a similar effect, since that wasn't included in the study.

COMFORTING

• **Swaddle your baby.** Many babies up to about two or three months love the feeling of being snugly contained, or swaddled. When young infants get upset, their arms and legs tend to flail around, which makes them even more overstimulated. Try holding your baby firmly but gently in your arms, or use a receiving blanket to wrap him up like a little package with his head sticking out, tight enough to keep his arms and legs contained, but not too tight (especially around the chest).

• **Use your face and voice to get your baby's attention.** If your baby is fussy, you might be able to divert him by entertaining him with your face and voice. Remember that young babies see best at a distance of about 9 to 12 inches. Bring your face within that range, and say something using a soft tone—you might even try sticking out your tongue. If your baby stops fussing to look and listen, you've got him!

• **Get your baby in motion.** Rhythmic motion is a time-honored way to calm a baby. Wind-up or battery-driven swings are often effective. But nothing beats your own living arms that come complete with your warmth, smell, and the sound of your heartbeat. If your baby is crying actively, you might want to start rocking at a more rapid pace, matching the rhythm of your baby's cries. Then, as you gradually slow down your rocking, the crying may slow along with it.

• **Get a move on.** Sometimes going for a ride is just the change of pace a fussy child needs to settle down, either in a stroller or in the car. Be careful, though, not to come to rely on a car ride to put your baby to sleep on a regular basis—he may become dependent on this habit. (See page 168 for some tips on choosing the proper car seat for your child.)

• **Sing soothing songs.** This is just a variation on the face-and-voice technique mentioned above. If you know any lullabies, sing those. If you don't, make up your own. For example, you might start with simply the word "baby," sung to a familiar melody. When you get tired of "baby," try singing about your day: "We got up early this morning/We had breakfast and went for a stroll." You don't have to be a great songwriter for your baby to be fascinated by your compositions.

• **Dance away your baby's blues.** This is a variation on rocking, only this time you're standing up and moving to music. It's important that you have a good, secure hold of your baby, and a space where you can move freely without bumping into anything. Babies, I've found, often have very particular tastes in music. Some favor Italian opera; others are more into Van Halen. Play different types to see which your little music-lover responds to best.

• **Experiment with different holding positions.** Every baby seems to have a preference in the way he likes to be held. Try different positions until you learn your child's personal favorites: Hold your baby in the crook of your arm (good for rocking). Place him upright, looking backward over your shoulder. Try laying him face down across your forearm. Put your baby in your lap looking up at you, legs and feet against your chest. Or

---

EASY RIDER: CHOOSING THE RIGHT CAR SEAT FOR YOUR CHILD

Whether you're taking your child for a ride to comfort her or just zipping off to Grandma's house, a good car seat, properly installed, is an essential piece of baby equipment. There are two main types of car seats for infants: rear-facing only and convertible seats. Most rear-facing infant seats have a 22-pound weight limit, but they do double duty as baby carriers. Convertible seats face backward for infants and young toddlers, then can be turned around to face forward for older toddlers and preschoolers. Don't get the type with shields or bars—they're not safe for young infants because their faces can hit the shield or bar in a crash; instead, look for a car seat with a harness.

Some important safety considerations:

• **Infants should always ride rear-facing in the back seat of the car.** *It is safe to switch to a front-facing position when your child is both 12 months of age or older and weighs 20 lbs. or more.*

lay him face down across your legs while you gently rub his back—babies seem to enjoy a bit of a massage now and then.

•*Not all car seats fit all cars.* Before you purchase a car seat, try it out in your car in the parking lot or make sure that you can return it if it doesn't fit properly.

•*Beware of used seats.* They cost less, but they may not be safe. Never use a seat that is more than 10 years old or has been in a crash—it could be weakened, even if it looks OK. Also, since you didn't send in the warranty card, you won't be notified by the manufacturer if there is a recall.

•*Keep in mind that installing a car seat properly is not easy.* In fact, four out of five parents get it wrong! Read both your car's manual and the instructions for the seat carefully. Then have a certified child safety seat inspector check that you have the right equipment and are using it correctly. Many fire stations and hospitals have trained technicians who provide this service for free. To find one, call your local fire department or hospital, or go to the National Highway Traffic Safety Administration's helpful and instructive website, www.nhtsa.dot.gov.

• **Do nothing.** This is actually one of the hardest things for many parents to do. If you've tried a few different soothing techniques and your baby is still fussy, it may be that he is simply overstimulated. The harder you try, the fussier he seems to get. To understand how your baby may be feeling, imagine yourself at the end of a hard day, when all you want is some peace and quiet, and there is an energetic and overly helpful person who keeps asking you what's wrong and trying to cheer you up. Sometimes what a baby really needs is to be left alone in a quiet, dark room, to fuss without interference until he falls asleep.

TODDLERS

As children move from infancy to toddlerhood, their emotions become more complex. Shame and jealousy emerge alongside sadness, anger, and fear. More and more, the goal of comforting is not just to soothe children's upsets, but also to address the underlying emotions, a feat made possible by their increasingly sophisticated understanding and use of language. Instead of just howling in rage, a three-year-old can say, "That's my doll!" At the same time, parents can use language to reassure her: "Don't worry, I won't let him take your doll away."

As the parent of a toddler, you'll also learn much more about your child's personality and patterns—what annoys her, what angers her, what makes her afraid. Often, you'll find that you can head off tantrums or tears by avoiding potentially upsetting situations (a sort of "pre-comforting," if you will). If your toddler has a hard time sharing toys, for example—which is perfectly natural and developmentally appropriate at this age—you might want to carry two shovels and pails to the sandbox at the local park, one for your child and one for anyone else who happens along. If experience teaches you that a late-afternoon trip to the grocery store is likely to result in a tearful or angry meltdown, you might be able to run your errands in the morning so you'll have an alert, sunny little co-shopper by your side. You'll find ways to use distraction and humor to ward off emotional outbursts, as well as tricks to keep boredom at bay. Your natural instinct is probably to keep introducing your toddler to new experiences, which is great—not only will she learn in leaps and bounds, but a child who can enjoy many different sorts of activities is likely to be more content in the long run.

Toddlers learn to talk the talk

One of the most important ways you can help your young child deal with negative emotions is to supply the words for him. Words allow a child to manage emotions without having to act them out first. In this way, language brings emotions under the control of reason. Consider the bright two-year-old who looks longingly at a big, friendly dog bounding by and sadly states, "All-gone doggy!" This mini-sentence clearly means, "That dog I wanted to play with just walked away!" You might reply, "You're sad because that dog went away." When you use the word "sad" to describe your child's emotions, you give him an important tool for dealing with sadness in the future. Now he has a name for that particular feeling when it occurs again, making it a little more familiar and manageable, and one that he can clearly communicate to others so they understand his plight. Words also help parents comfort their children when they're fearful. Say, for instance, that far from being sad when the dog trots off, your toddler is relieved because he's afraid of dogs. He may need you to say, "You're OK, don't worry, that doggy is a nice doggy!" many times before he feels brave enough to risk a lick on the hand. It may take a long time for your comforting words to sink in, but eventually they probably will. (Of course, you can overdo the labeling of emotions, too. Children need to be able to feel what they feel without being subject to a constant running commentary. So here, as with so many aspects of parenting, you need to find a good balance.)

Separation anxiety can strike the boldest toddler
Between about 20 and 24 months, many toddlers go through a period of increased fearfulness. In particular, they seem to fear being separated from their parents and becoming lost. You know that your toddler is in this phase when you realize that she has become attached to your leg with invisible super-glue. She will not let you out of her sight. You do not have a moment alone, even in the bathroom.

There is no quick fix for this problem. An older toddler's clinginess comes, I think, from her realization that she is truly a separate person. She can imagine the possibility of being alone. Part of her even wants to be alone, independent, her own boss. And, of course, as exciting as it is, that idea is very, very frightening.

There is a magical children's book about this emotional tug-of-war called *The Runaway Bunny*. The author is Margaret Wise Brown, the same genius who wrote *Goodnight Moon*. Another classic that speaks to the same theme is *The Tale of Peter Rabbit* by Beatrix Potter. Reading these stories to your toddler may be reassuring. You also can make up your own stories about brave little creatures who wander far from home but manage to find their way back safely. Most important, your own confidence that this clingy phase really will pass (honest, it will!) will help your toddler—and you—make it through these months.

Parents help keep the monsters at bay

Around age two, children begin realize that the world is big, and that they are small. They know it can be dangerous out there, and that sometimes they are alone. This may be one reason why almost every child conjures up monsters to be afraid of, as I mentioned in the first chapter on sleeping. It may be less scary to deal with a monster that you have created, and therefore know something about, than to face a whole huge world full of forces that you don't understand at all.

Of course, young children have a hard time telling what's real from what's imaginary. They simply don't have enough experience with what is, and what is not, possible in the real world. When watching Dorothy and her friends being carried off to the wicked witch's palace

FEARS AND THE MEDIA

Thanks to the media, the average American child witnesses thousands of murders each year, as well as countless beatings, explosions, and other violent acts. It is very difficult for young children to sort out the real from the fictional, to know what is threatening and what isn't, and to feel safe in the face of so much violence. That's why I think you can't be too careful about the TV shows, websites, movies, and video games your child sees.

Parents sometimes feel their children need to be "toughened up to face the real world," and therefore need to be exposed to the ugliest and most violent aspects of our modern culture. I think this is a mistake. Children who are exposed to violent images too early do not become tough, they become numb. What's more, viewing violence makes children more prone to acting out violently, at least in the short run.

The American Academy of Pediatrics recommends that children under age two years not watch TV at all, and that older children watch no more than one to two hours a day. I would include videotapes and video games in these totals. Another wise policy is to watch along with your child, so you'll be there to explain and deflect any disturbing images.

in *The Wizard of Oz*, for example, how can a three-year-old be certain that evil flying monkeys don't exist, even when his mother tells him that it's "only a movie"?

Children are also proud. They demand that their fears, as well as their other ideas, be taken seriously. Teasing a young child for being frightened will make him feel ashamed, but it won't take care of the fears. Telling him, "There's nothing to be afraid of," is likely only to confuse him. A monster *is* something. It just happens to be an imaginary something.

The most helpful approach, I think, is to consistently help your child sort out what's real from what's imaginary. Let him know that you understand that imaginary things are important. But you also know that imaginary monsters really can't hurt him. It takes a long time for young children to truly grasp this distinction, so you need to be patient and repeat yourself as often as necessary.

Toddlers have tantrums for different reasons

It's surprisingly hard to define exactly what "temper tantrum" means. For some children, it means falling to the floor, kicking and screaming; for others, it may mean throwing toys, or even hitting and biting. Difficult as it is to define, most parents know a tantrum when they see it.

Maybe you think that the topic of tantrums belongs in a section on discipline, not comforting. And, certainly, when your toddler throws herself to the floor in the supermarket, yelling at the top of her lungs, it's understandable if your first impulse isn't to comfort her! Our children's temper tantrums often embarrass us, and

_____ **"** _____

PARENT TO PARENT
"When my daughter started having tantrums, I learned not to try to rationalize with her or use explanations she just couldn't understand. Instead, I'd try to validate her feelings. An example: My daughter loves shoes (scary, huh?). She was throwing a tantrum because she didn't want to leave the shoe department. I said, 'You love shoes, don't you? It's hard to leave when you want something so much. Mommy loves shoes, too.' She said, 'Uh-huh, OK, Mom,' and we left. End of tantrum. This approach has worked for me repeatedly."

— **jeremysmom,** AS POSTED ON DRSPOCK.COM

_____

ignite feelings of frustration, resentment, and anger. It's easy to forget that the screaming child at our feet is not being manipulative or "bad," but is, in fact, upset.

Children have temper tantrums for a variety of reasons. Some toddlers and preschoolers do use tantrums as a form of blackmail to get what they want. One hint that you have such a manipulative tyrant on your hands is that the tantrums stop the minute you give in, revealing a happy, self-satisfied child. But such a child is never really happy, because what she craves, beyond the toy or treat of the moment, is power. She feels loved and secure only when she is in charge, and the feeling does not last long. That's why I say that she is not just "bad," but also, in some sense, upset. What this child needs isn't comforting, exactly, but firm limits together with plenty of love that is not expressed through anything bought in a store.

Fortunately, most toddlers don't use tantrums for such deep, dark purposes. They simply fall apart emotionally when they are overwhelmed by fatigue, frustration, or fear. They can't tell you what they want. In fact, young children often break down precisely because they can't decide what they want, or when what they want is impossible. A one-year-old wants to be completely independent *and* she wants to be protected. A two-year-old wants to wear her red pajamas *and* her blue ones. A three-year-old wants a playmate *and* she wants all the toys to herself.

Fear as a cause of tantrums is not that common, except perhaps in a medical setting. In my office, I see children losing control fairly regularly when confronted with what they perceive as menacing equipment—ear probes, tongue depressors, and, of course, needles. Most parents realize that their child's screaming and flailing is not really bad behavior, but only fear and the instinct for self-preservation taking over. Still, they appreciate it when I understand and react with sympathy, rather than annoyance.

Practical tips

• **Use words to describe what your child is feeling.** "I know you feel mad" (as your child pounds the floor). "You look really frustrated" (as he throws his toy across the room). As children get older, they learn to use words rather than actions to express their emotions. Before they can do that, they need to hear those feeling words—"sad," "mad," "frustrated," "tired"—spoken many, many times by their parents.

• **Keep your child safe, but don't interfere if you don't have to.** If your child has a meltdown on a concrete floor, you may have to pick him up and move him onto a soft surface so that he doesn't bruise himself. If he seems intent on banging his head, hard, you may need to hold him to keep him safe. Otherwise, you don't necessarily have to take action.

• **Move away, but stay within view.** A young child's biggest fear is that he will be left alone, abandoned by his parents. If you walk out of sight while your child is having a tantrum, he might become even more scared and upset. He may think, I'm so bad, I made my mommy (or daddy) go away. It's better if your child knows that you're there nearby, even if you are not looking at him or talking to him.

• **Tell your child that you're sure he'll feel better when he's done feeling upset.** This statement expresses your confidence that things will not always be as upsetting as they seem at the moment. For a young child, the present feels like forever, especially when he's miserable. Your confidence that there is a brighter future, maybe just minutes away, can be very helpful.

• **Keep your cool.** Intense attention from a parent is rewarding for a young child, whether it comes in the form of pleading, offers of rewards, or angry yelling and threats of punishment—in other words, whether the behavior results in positive or negative parental attention. And any behavior that is rewarded tends to happen more often. So, by giving their children lots of attention, parents often make tantrums last longer and come on more frequently.

Classic Spock

"If you can tell that a tantrum is in the offing, try distraction: 'Oh. Look at that birdie. He's flying. Let's go see.' If you're very lucky, the child's attention will be deflected from the frustrating circumstance at hand and will move on to something else. Distraction is always worth a try—but don't get your hopes up that it will always work."

— Dr. Benjamin Spock, *Baby and Child Care*

179

• **Don't change your mind because of a tantrum.** After some parents make a certain decision—say, telling their children that they can't have ice cream right now—they sometimes stand firm and sometimes change their minds if their offspring pitch a fit. Mistake, big mistake. If children find out that crying and screaming may get them what they want, they often learn to throw more and longer tantrums, in hopes that this will be one of the times their parents give in.

• **Once the tantrum's done, let your child know that you are proud of him for having gotten himself back under control.** After a particularly trying tantrum, it's completely understandable that you would feel like venting your own frustration by giving your child a good scolding. But hold back. It's not easy for a child to pull himself together after a really big tantrum. Give him credit. Look forward to future successes, saying something like, "Next time when you're upset, I bet you won't have to yell for as long before you feel OK again."

• **Try to lower the general level of stress your child is feeling.** Make sure that he is getting enough sleep. Get treatment for any ongoing medical problems, such as allergies or chronic ear infections. If he's in daycare or preschool, are you sure he feels safe and happy there? Are there conflicts in your home that involve a lot of yelling or fighting?

• **Think about specific triggers that seem to bring on tantrums.** Do the tantrums often occur when your child is tired or hungry, or when you are? Do certain circumstances seem to bring on the tantrums, such as crowds, new people, or stores full of enticing things? Which of these things can you change? For example, rather than taking your toddler to the park at 4 P.M., when everyone is tired and hungry, try to go in the morning, or at least carry a snack with you.

Special Situations

CHILDREN WHO ARE HARD TO SOOTHE

Maybe you've tried all the techniques mentioned in this book, as well as a few innovative ones of your own, and still find your child very hard to soothe. No matter what you do, your baby still cries often and for a long, long time. Or maybe your toddler is extremely timid and fearful when confronted with new people, places, or situations despite your tireless efforts to make her more confident and outgoing. There are many different traits that can make a child difficult to soothe. It's important to know about these, because blaming yourself never helps and recognizing the special character of your child can help you find more effective comforting approaches. The following list is not complete, but it includes many of the more common causes:

• **Irregular biological rhythms.** If a young child's cycles of hunger and tiredness are fairly regular, you can often guess what's upsetting her just by knowing her patterns and what time of day it is. But when a child's biological rhythms are highly irregular, it can be very hard to know what to do when.

• **Hypersensitivity.** Occasionally, a child may be very sensitive to sound, so that normal amounts of background noise are very irritating to her. Another child may have a similar sensitivity in the visual area, and be overstimulated by the play of light and shadow on her nursery wall on a sunny day (a translucent window shade can help in this case). Still another child may be oversensitive to touch, so that light stroking of the skin is actually very uncomfortable for her. Many children like this feel better when they are swaddled, or held with gentle but firm pressure.

• **Low or high muscle tone.** A child with low muscle tone, who is not able to sit up on her own by seven months or reach effectively for toys, may experience constant frustration and a sense of helplessness. A child with very high tone, whose muscles are constantly active and whose body is constantly in motion, may have a hard time relaxing and calming down.

• **High intensity of responding.** Some children express their emotions with an unusually high amount of energy. When they're happy, they're gleeful; when they're sad, they're miserable. A child who has this temperamental trait can be hard to soothe, just because her negative emotions are so powerfully expressed.

• **Medical problems.** Children who are being treated for temporary medical problems, such as colds or earaches, can be difficult to soothe because they are in pain. Chronic conditions, such as cerebral palsy, asthma, and recurring ear infections, also involve ongoing discomfort that can undermine a parent's efforts to offer comfort.

• **Developmental problems.** Rarely, resistance to being soothed is the first sign of a serious developmental problem such as autism. Often there are other signs, too, such as a lack of eye contact and interest in other people's (e.g., mother's) emotional states.

If you suspect that your child has any of these or other traits that make it hard for you to give comfort, you may be able to make a small change—for example, keeping her room quieter and darker—that will help a great deal. You also may want to get help from a professional. A good place to start is with your child's doctor. From there, a referral to a child psychologist or developmental-behavioral pediatrician may give you peace of mind by assuring you that there is no serious problem or, if one is identified, help you plan a course of action to deal with it.

COLIC

Roughly 1 in 10 babies cries much longer or more intensely than the average. When this crying is severe enough to cause parents to worry or to feel powerless, frustrated, or angry, it's called colic. If you read other things about colic, you might come across the classic definition of "crying for three or more hours a day, three or more days per week." This definition is useful for research. But in the real world, some babies cry for less than three hours, but their screams are intense and piercing, and their parents are justifiably frantic. These babies have colic. Other babies spend more time engaged in low-level fussing, but don't cause their parents much worry. I don't consider these babies to have colic.

In most infants who develop colic, the frequent or intense crying usually starts around three or four weeks of age and often gets worse before it gets better. Although parents may find it hard to believe when they find themselves in its frustrating, heart-breaking, and very noisy clutches, colic is a temporary problem. Nine out of 10 colicky babies outgrow the condition by three or four months of age. For the most part, they are not any fussier or more difficult as toddlers and preschoolers than children who didn't have colic.

Colic occurs in healthy babies

While they are crying, babies with colic certainly appear to be miserable. However, in general, they are healthy and continue to grow and develop normally. In fact, most doctors now believe that colic isn't a disease, it's a malfunction of a basically healthy organ system—what we call a functional problem. For example, the baby's intestines might churn in a poorly coordinated fashion, causing cramping. The intestines themselves are healthy, but they aren't functioning up to par. A temporary over-sensitivity to noises or visual stimulation also can result in colic. There's nothing really wrong with the baby's brain; it's just immature and not ready to handle everything that the world is throwing its way. A sleep disorder is another type of functional problem that occasionally seems to cause colic.

It's very hard to do a test that proves that a functional problem is to blame for the excessive crying. Therefore, when presented with a baby with apparent colic, a doctor will first try to rule out other, more serious medical conditions. Here are some of the things he will look for:

• **The baby is growing normally.** Serious problems with the digestive system or the processes that provide energy and remove waste products are likely to result in poor growth. Normal growth (described in Chapter 2) is a good sign that basic body functions are working well.

• **The excessive crying takes place mostly during a particular time of day, usually in the evening.** Medical illnesses don't typically turn off completely for a part of the day, although they may be a bit better or worse at different times. A baby whose pattern is to be happy and active from sunup until sundown and then start fussing inconsolably is not likely to have a medical illness.

• **The baby's physical examination is normal.** A thorough physical examination does not completely rule out all medical problems that might cause excessive crying, but it does eliminate quite a few. For example, a baby may have a tiny scratch on the surface of one eye, causing lots of pain and fussing. A careful exam by the doctor could find the scratch, and treatment with a soothing ointment would cure the "colic."

• **Laboratory tests come up negative.** Most doctors consider that if a baby's medical history and physical examination are reassuring, then blood tests or X rays aren't likely to add anything. On the other hand, if there are signs in your child's history or physical exam pointing to a particular disease, then it makes sense to do specific tests to confirm or rule out that diagnosis. (A doctor's reluctance to just automatically run a lot of tests can frustrate some parents. The problem is, the tests themselves carry problems and risks—pain from the needle to draw blood, for instance, or radiation from X rays—and they are expensive. Most important, almost all of the tests are sure to come back "normal," telling you nothing for all that effort and expense. Doing a lot of tests without guidance from the medical history or examination doesn't help, and may well do harm. It's just bad medicine.)

Comfort measures for a colicky baby
From folkloric remedies to prescription medicines, there are hundreds of ways to treat colic, but there is no one magic bullet. What works for one baby may not work for another. The suggestions below are ones I've found most helpful in my own practice. See which make sense to you, and give them a try.

**Mom's medicines
can make a baby feel ill** 🐛

*One often-overlooked cause of colicky-type crying
is a negative reaction to a mother's medications.
If you are nursing, any substances you take are
likely to pass into your breast milk. Sometimes
medicines that are perfectly fine for an adult can
cause problems in a baby and make her feel
miserable. Just one more reason to be sure to talk
with your doctor—and your child's—if you're taking any medications while you're breastfeeding.*

• **Get medical reassurance.** The fear that your baby
might really be sick is bound to make his crying a hundred times harder to endure. So your first step should be
to have your baby thoroughly evaluated by his doctor.
After the initial evaluation, you and the doctor should
be in frequent contact, and the doctor should see your
baby regularly—every week or two—to make sure that
your infant still is healthy (despite the crying).

• **Reduce stimulation.** One of the main causes of colic
is overstimulation. If you notice that your baby
becomes more upset and frantic the more you try to
calm him down, that can be a clue that you need to do
less, not more. Lower the lights. Make the room as
quiet as you can. Swaddle your baby, so that his arm

DISEASES THAT APPEAR TO BE COLIC 🐜

True colic is not a disease, and most babies with colic are not sick. But many different diseases can cause excessive crying and might appear to be colic at first glance. In particular, there are three medical conditions that are likely to cause pain and colic-like crying:

*• **Milk protein allergy.** As I've explained in Chapter 2, it's common for infants to be allergic to proteins found in formulas made from cow's milk. Many babies also are allergic to proteins in soy-based formulas. Allergies to infant formula can cause rashes or even small amounts of bleeding into the intestines, detectable with a simple, in-office medical test. But sometimes a baby's excessive crying is the only apparent symptom. If allergies are causing the crying and you're using formula, changing to a so-called "elemental" or hypoallergenic variety can help you make the diagnosis and treat the disease all in one step. If you're nursing your baby, consider removing all dairy and soy from your diet, since the proteins make their way into the breast milk.*

*• **Lactose intolerance.** This is another condition that can cause bloating, discomfort, and colicky*

crying after a milk meal (see Chapter 2). The
baby's body simply can't absorb a particular sugar,
lactose. The lactose remains in the intestines,
where it ferments, causing gassy cramping and
diarrhea. Babies commonly develop lactose
intolerance for a period of days or weeks following
a mild bout of infectious diarrhea, and a small
number have permanent lactose intolerance.
Soy formulas, and some special cow's-milk
formulas, are lactose free. Switching to one of
these formulas can make a big difference if your
baby's "colic" is really an inability to digest lactose.

• **Gastroesophageal reflux disease (GERD).**
Also described in the last chapter, GERD causes
stomach acid to squirt back up into the
esophagus, causing severe heartburn. A little bit
of this reflux is normal in babies, but when it
occurs frequently, the stomach acid can damage
the esophagus, resulting in a lot of pain. Reflux is
often worst several minutes after eating, when
the stomach is full, especially if the baby is lying
flat. Crying that regularly occurs after a baby
fills up on milk suggests GERD. Arching of the
back and stiffening, both responses to acid in the
esophagus, are other signs. Treatment for GERD,
including special feeding techniques and perhaps
medications, is often very effective.

and leg movements don't add to the level of stimulation. Talk softly, or not at all. Lay your baby down on his back in his cradle or crib. If you feel comfortable, leave the room. Very often, a colicky baby will fuss for a while, then fall asleep, which is what he really needs.

• **Battle boredom.** Now that I've told you to reduce the stimulation your baby encounters, it may seem contradictory to urge you to "battle boredom." But it's not really as perverse as it seems. Too little stimulation can be just as uncomfortable for children as too much; they are born with the drive to learn new things and become fretful if they're not properly challenged and entertained. The trick is to strike a balance, depending on your child's development and temperament. Respect his need for downtime, but when he seems to be in an alert, receptive mood, be ready to talk, sing, and play with him. A newborn also may be fascinated by mobiles, shadows, older siblings, and other things that move and change. Older babies love to explore their own bodies. Around four or five months, simple toys that they can grasp, bang, stack, and put in their mouths are enough to keep them happily entertained for a while.

• **Make changes to your baby's formula or your diet.** Some pediatricians discourage making formula changes in response to colic, but the evidence is solid and convincing: Changing to a lactose-free, non-dairy, non-soy formula (an elemental formula, described in Chapter 2) works a fair amount of the time. It's easier to make this change and see what happens than to order expensive tests for food allergy or lactose intolerance.

If you are nursing, try removing all dairy and soy from your diet, since cow's-milk and soy proteins do pass into breast milk. (Remember, however, to consume other sources of important nutrients like calcium and protein.) Other dietary changes also can make a big difference. Try cutting out all caffeine-containing drinks and foods: coffee, tea, many soft drinks (not just colas), and chocolate (alas!). Also eliminate cabbage, Brussels sprouts, broccoli, and similar vegetables that cause gas. Many babies like the taste of garlic in milk, but try to cut down on strong spices, especially hot peppers.

If you are lucky and your baby's crying decreases within a few days of your making these changes, that's wonderful. But it does not mean that your baby is actually allergic or lactose intolerant. Since colic sometimes goes away on its own, and since making any change at all can sometimes reduce a baby's crying, you can't be sure that taking away cow's protein or lactose is what did the trick. It makes sense, therefore, to wait a few weeks and then gradually reintroduce the old formula (or start eating small amounts of dairy yourself, if you're breastfeeding and you like milk, cheese, and ice cream). Chances are pretty good that your baby will do just fine with this diet the second time around. If not, you haven't done any harm. Either way, you've found out something important about your baby.

• **Watch your baby's bottle-feeding habits.** If your baby seems gassy (which he might show by habitually fussing after meals and being relieved partially by a big burp), one cause might be swallowed air. Every baby swallows at least a little air along with the formula he drinks, but too much can cause distress. To help keep your infant from swallowing too much air, always tilt the bottle at an angle that keeps the nipple full of formula while he is sucking. If you notice that your baby has to suck very vigorously to get the formula out, try widening the hole in the nipple using a heated pin. If your baby gets lots of milk with each suck and ends up gulping, try changing to a nipple with a smaller hole. Give your baby a chance to burp if he needs to, keeping in mind that vigorous patting, rubbing, and jostling actually don't help babies burp better. Two positions that seem to help babies get rid of extra air in the stomach are sitting up on your lap leaning slightly forward, or held upright against your chest looking over your shoulder. (If you cover your shoulder with a cloth diaper first, you won't have to change your own clothes as often after burping your baby.)

• **Try using a baby carrier.** Most scientific studies have failed to prove that carrying a baby around for most of the day, as is common in some cultures, actually wards off colic. However, using a cloth sling or a soft front-pack is still a lovely way to stay close. Physical contact reduces crying for many babies, and it may also have positive effects on their emotional development. In my mind, a cloth chest-pack is miles better than one of those hard plastic baby seats with a handle that seem to be so popular. Not only is your baby closer to you—

all you have to do is tip your head down to kiss the top of his head!—but your hands are free, as well.

• **Experiment with motion and vibration.** If riding in the car calms your baby, you might want to invest in a vibrator that attaches to the crib and creates a similarly soothing motion. Some parents place their babies in a baby seat on top of the clothes dryer. If you do this, I'd suggest using duct tape to attach the seat securely to the dryer; otherwise, the seat can easily vibrate right off the dryer and crash onto the floor. Baby swings work for some babies, but often only for a short time. Be sure your baby is safely belted in, and that the swing itself is sturdy and stable.

• **Try using music, white noise, and other soothing sounds.** You can buy tapes of a human heartbeat, the sound of the wind sighing through trees, and the melodious tinkle of a babbling brook. You can also buy a white-noise generator, although a cheap radio tuned in to a low buzz of static may do the trick. None of these things have been proven effective in research tests, but they do seem to help soothe some babies—and they can't hurt.

• **Serve your baby a little herbal tea.** Given in small quantities, mild herbal teas, such as chamomile, verbena, or mint, help calm some babies. Beware of teas that contain caffeine. Avoid giving your baby a large quantity of tea or any other clear liquid, since it's likely to take the place of formula or breast milk, which is

193

much more nutritious. Excessive intake of clear liquids such as tea also can cause dangerous changes in a baby's blood chemistry. As a good rule of thumb, you're safe if you give no more than about four ounces in any 24-hour period.

• **Ask your doctor before resorting to medications for colic.** It is very tempting to turn to medications to treat colic, but it is usually not a good solution. Medications containing simethicone that promise to relieve gas in the stomach have been shown to be no more effective than sugar water. Other medications are actually dangerous. Medications that are supposed to reduce intestinal cramping (anti-spasmodics) also can reduce the drive to breathe. Some medications contain alcohol or drugs that are close relatives to opium; they can cause oversedation and other grim side effects. Even acetaminophen (the main ingredient in Tylenol and some other pain- and fever-reducing medicines) is dangerous if given in large quantities or for too many days in a row. Aspirin should never be given to children because of the risk of serious liver damage (Reye syndrome.) Of course, if there is a medical disease causing a child to cry (that is, if the crying is not due to colic), then your baby's doctor might prescribe medication to treat that specific disease.

• **Massage your baby.** Premature babies grow better if they get regular massages, and massage helps with many stress-related conditions in older children and adults, too. Unfortunately, I know of little evidence that it helps infants with colic. Still, it's worth a try. There are licensed massage therapists, but I think that any gentle, rhythmic touching is bound to be beneficial. A warm water bottle (caution: not hot!) placed over your infant's belly is another traditional, but not proven, remedy.

• **Quit smoking.** Smoking during pregnancy may increase the likelihood of a baby's developing colic, and exposure to secondhand smoke after birth may bring colic on. Of course, there are many other excellent reasons to stop smoking. Secondhand smoke increases a baby's risk of developing asthma, pneumonia, and ear infections, among other things. And, of course, it puts your own life at risk from heart disease, stroke, and cancer.

Coping with colic

I've already assured you that colic doesn't last forever. But knowing that colic eventually passes doesn't make it "all better" for the parents. For many, weeks of what seems like nonstop crying is literally torture. Under this stress, many parents develop symptoms of depression or anxiety; sometimes their marriages even suffer. Many actually fantasize about hurting their babies, and then may feel ashamed or frightened by these feelings. As a result, their confidence as parents can falter. Colicky crying drives some people, even a few parents and caregivers, to commit child abuse—for example, by shaking a baby. As awful as this is, it is understandable, in a way. Colic can make adults feel they have to do something, anything, to make it stop.

195

COMFORTING

I don't say this to scare you, but to reassure you that if your baby has colic and you find yourself stressed to the breaking point, you should know that you are not alone. Many wonderful parents have suffered greatly with colic. It can be one of the hardest things a parent endures, particularly if it lasts past the usual three-to-four-month end-point. For some relief, be sure to work with your child's pediatrician and try the suggestions I give for coping with colic. On the positive side, if you can make it through colic, you can probably make it through anything!

• **Don't blame yourself.** Remind yourself that colic is not your fault, it's not a sign that your baby is sick, and you're doing everything you can. Excellent parents often have colicky babies. If family members, in-laws, friends, or colleagues suggest otherwise, ignore them. They don't know what they're talking about.

• **Give yourself an occasional break.** Find someone you trust to look after your baby while you go out for a while and just relax. If you are exhausted all of the time, you won't be able to enjoy your baby, and you won't be as effective at calming her down as you would otherwise be.

As important as this concept is, I have to add a word of warning. As I mentioned above, it takes a great deal of patience to be with a screaming baby, as you well know. Many cases of serious child abuse result when a person who is not the baby's parent is left to care for a colicky infant. Often, it is a boyfriend who

Q: Our first baby had colic for four months, and it took a long time for us to be brave enough to get pregnant again. But now we're expecting our second child. What are the chances that we'll have to go through the same thing with this baby?

A: Once you've had a colicky baby, it is completely understandable that you never want to go through that again. I don't think the risk of having a second colicky baby is high. One scientific report I consulted noted that it is common for one child in a family to have colic, while the other children do not. This squares with my experience taking care of children with colic, as well. People wonder about various factors influencing colic, but the chances of a baby's developing colic seem to be the same whether a baby is full term or premature, male or female, first born or later born, nursed or bottle-fed.

shakes the baby to quiet her down, and in the process causes serious brain damage. If there is any question in your mind about the ability of your helper to handle the stress, it is wise to stay in your home, even if you allow your helper to do the baby care for a few hours. That way, you are there in case you are needed. Anyone caring for your child must understand that it is *never* safe to shake a baby.

• **Don't be afraid to ask for support and guidance.** If you ever feel yourself at the end of your rope—and this happens to many, many parents who have a colicky baby at home—then you need to ask for help. There is no shame whatsoever in letting your spouse, partner, friends, or doctor know that you simply cannot take it anymore. Often, just having a sympathetic person to talk with can help a lot. Sometimes professional counseling can help boost your coping abilities to get you through an especially rough time. Another option is to call your local child-abuse or parenting hotlines. Simply dial 411 and ask for the county child protection agency, or call 911 and ask for help. You don't have to worry that they'll think you're a monster or try to take your baby away from you. But they may be able to help with what's known as respite care, in which a well-meaning person takes care of your baby temporarily, giving you a chance to recover your emotional strength.

Certainly, if you think that you might actually harm your child out of frustration or anger, then you need to call someone right away. Parents are often afraid to ask for assistance in this way, but they shouldn't be. Getting help when you need it, even though you may be scared, shows how much you truly love your baby.

• **Alert your neighbors.** Sometimes one of the more uncomfortable aspects of colic is the concern that your neighbors are being disturbed or, worse yet, are passing judgment on your parenting. I've found that a direct approach often helps in this case. Knock on your neighbors' doors and explain that your baby has colic. Explain that you've been to the doctor, you're trying a bunch of things, and you know that the crying won't last forever. But in the meantime, you hope your neighbors aren't too disturbed by the racket. Almost always, this sort of open explanation meets with sympathy, friendly reassurance, and smiles when you pass in the hallways or on the street.

GRIEF

Up to this point, I've been talking about providing comfort for everyday upsets. Grief—the emotional response to a serious loss—is a different kind of distress. Grief doesn't happen every day, of course. But neither does it pass by quickly, like the pain of a skinned knee or the ache of a broken bone. Grief, of course, is a part of life. But many adults are uncomfortable with the idea that even very young children—infants and toddlers!—sometimes experience grief. And because young children often cannot express their feelings in words, it may not be obvious when a child is grieving and needs help.

As a parent, you need to be able to recognize grief and the events that bring it on. Once you understand the special ways in which young children experience loss, you may be able to protect your child from some sources of sorrow. And if losses are unavoidable, you may be able to see your child's grief for what it is, and respond in ways that can bring comfort.

Grief can spring from many sources

In young children, the main cause of grief is the loss of an important relationship. Loss can occur when a parent, grandparent, or sibling dies, of course. But, for a young child, even a short separation from a loved one can trigger the experience of loss. By short, I mean a separation of as little as a week or two. Here are some examples of situations that can cause babies and toddlers to grieve:

• The parents of a 10-month-old decide to take a vacation, leaving their baby in the care of grandparents she doesn't know well.

• An 18-month-old is hospitalized for a ruptured appendix, and has to receive antibiotics in the hospital for two weeks. Unfortunately, his mother lives far away and has other children at home, and she has no car. So once she sees him through the operation, she doesn't come back until it is time to pick him up.

• A three-year-old wakes to find out that her mother is gone, rushed to the hospital with a serious blood disorder. After a week, the child is allowed to visit, but the woman lying in the hospital bed does not look like her mother.

Notice that in each of these cases, a young child is separated from her parent or parents for a period of several days. Also, there is a lack of support from other trusted adults. In the first example, the grandparent who comes to take care of the child was really a stranger. In the second case, the child was surrounded by nurses and doctors who were all strangers, and who kept changing every shift. And in the third case, we can imagine that the father was frantically worried about his wife, at the hospital all day, and not as available to offer enough reassurance and support to his child.

Even very young children feel grief

Before about seven or eight months of age, it is fairly easy for babies to substitute one loving caregiver for another. They don't seem to have much ability to miss a person who is no longer there, as long as there is somebody else present who meets their needs. For this reason, very young babies may be somewhat protected from grief that comes from separation.

Between about 8 and 10 months, however, babies change. They become much less accepting of strangers, for example, and often protest more when parents leave them with babysitters, even ones they know. They are also much less willing to accept comforting from anyone but their parents or other trusted adults.

Once babies have reached this developmental stage, they become very vulnerable to grief, and remain so through the toddler years. For one thing, it's hard to reassure a young child that her mommy or daddy will come back, because, of course, she can't understand what you're saying. Also, time passes more slowly for babies. Because they can't easily imagine the future or recall the past, the present seems to last forever. So, even short separations can feel as though they are permanent.

201

Sometimes the signs can be subtle

Before you can comfort a grieving child, you have to recognize that he is feeling grief. A grieving adult looks sad, wears dark clothes, and stops going out; his sorrow and pain are obvious. A grieving toddler may mix periods of sadness with periods of normal-looking behavior, including laughing and playing. Grief in a toddler may look like physical illness, with irritability, listlessness, poor appetite and even vomiting. Or, it may look like bad behavior, with frequent tantrums, destructiveness, or aggressiveness. (At all ages, grief includes a mix of emotions, including both sadness and anger, so it shouldn't be too surprising that toddlers sometimes act out these complex feelings, too.)

In young children, grief does not manifest itself instantly; it develops over time. Young children who are separated from their parents, like the 18-month-old who found himself alone in the hospital, pass through three stages of grief:

• **Stage 1: Protest.** Right after a child experiences a loss, he's likely to show a great deal of upset. He cries bitterly, throws temper tantrums, pleads for his mother to return, or tries to go after her. He refuses to be comforted, and may stop eating.

• **Stage 2: Despair.** After several days of protest, the child calms down. He begins to eat, and perhaps to play a bit. Much of the time, though, he may appear sad or serious, and he may glance longingly at the place where he last saw his departed parent. He no longer calls out or tries to follow. Eventually, he may begin to behave fairly normally.

• **Stage 3: Detachment and Long-Term Effects.** If the absent parent returns after the child has passed through Stages 1 and 2, the child may not greet her with joy. Instead, he turns his head away, and refuses to recognize her, or he clenches his fists and strikes out at her. Once at home, he may remain distant or angry for days or weeks. Or his behavior may shift to extreme clinginess. He panics if his mother is out of sight, even for an instant, refuses to sleep alone, and throws violent tantrums if his mother tries to go anywhere without him. A different child, with a less expressive temperament, acts withdrawn or anxious, frequently looking up to make sure that his mother has not disappeared.

This sequence of events is typical for young children who are separated from their parent or parents for a period of several days or longer. In the 1950s in England, a series of films was made of children who were hospitalized without their parents. Watching these young children go through this process of protest, despair, and detachment is heart wrenching.

Largely as a result of those films, hospital policies changed. Parents were no longer sent home, but were invited to stay, and eventually hospitals even began to provide places for them to sleep. I feel so strongly about parents' staying with their young children in the hospital that I do not shy away from making parents feel guilty if I think it will persuade them to stay. If parents truly must leave, then I recommend that they visit as frequently as possible. Parents sometimes stay away because they don't want their babies to have to say goodbye again and again. But I am certain that multiple goodbyes are far easier on a young child than is the process of grieving for a parent's seemingly permanent loss.

Helping a child cope with separation

Telling you about the grief your child might experience during a separation isn't intended to make you feel guilty. Parents sometimes have to leave their children in someone else's care temporarily because of a business trip, a much-needed vacation, or other valid reasons. The point is to be aware of how your child views such separations and to make it a little easier on her to bear. Here are some things you can do.

• **Separations are easier when your baby's very young.** If your baby is younger than eight months old, as I mentioned above, she is unlikely to miss you too much if she is well cared for by someone else. Make sure that she is tended by a competent, affectionate, patient person who is familiar with her feeding, sleeping, and other routines. Grandparents, aunts or uncles, or close family members usually are the best choices and probably will cherish this chance to spend special one-on-one time with a beloved baby.

• **Leave her with someone familiar.** Once an infant reaches the age of eight months or so, try to leave her with someone she knows (and likes) very well. This person should be kind, attentive, and competent—and able to keep up with your young child's activity level (toddlers, especially, require an energetic and ever-vigilant caregiver). Again, try to ensure that the caregiver will stick to your child's normal routines as much as possible.

• **Check in often.** Even if they have a child old enough to talk on the phone (or at least recognize and enjoy the sounds of their mom or dad's voice), some parents think it's kinder not to call often while they're away, thinking it just reminds the child that she misses her parents. However, I think it's actually much harder on a child for days to go by without hearing from her parents. If possible, try to call your older baby or toddler every day or so, and be upbeat and loving, stressing that you miss her and will, indeed, return very soon (if that's the truth!).

• **When you return, don't be surprised or hurt if it takes a while for your child to warm up to you again.** Let her know that the absence was hard for you, too, and how happy you are to be together again. You don't have to make a big fuss or do anything special; in fact, getting back to your familiar routines as quickly as possible is the best thing you can do for your child's peace of mind. If your child's behavior doesn't return to normal after a few weeks, or if it is truly alarming to you for any amount of time, talk with your child's doctor or with a professional who knows about children's emotional development, such as a child psychologist or developmental-behavioral pediatrician. A child's grief can be very hard for a parent to deal with; there's no reason you have to do this alone.

The loss of a parent is especially devastating

Dealing with a parent's temporary absence is one thing. Dealing with losing a parent permanently, through death or a sudden sharp separation, is another. (The effects of losing a grandparent, a sibling, or even a babysitter or favorite uncle may be similar or different, depending on the child's relationship with that person.)

It's safe to assume that any child who has suffered the loss of a parent or a parent-figure will experience emotional pain and will need help to get through the experience. There really is no such thing as a child's simply being "fine" after such a loss, even if the child doesn't show outward signs of grief. In fact, I worry more about children who seem all right, because they may not know how to express their feelings and therefore may not get the help they need. The same, I think, goes for the remaining parent; it's simply asking too much of yourself to expect to deal with the loss alone. If you have a good support system—family, friends, a religious community, or professionals you trust—let these people help you. Even if you are a strong person, one who never wants to show any weakness or ask for help, consider the possibility that, under certain circumstances, seeking support and guidance may be a sign of true strength.

There is no simple prescription for helping a child through grief. Every child's experience is unique. But there are some general principles that apply:

• **Next to missing the parent who has died, the greatest stress for a young child is the fear that the other parent also will disappear.** He needs to hear that you, the remaining parent, are not going to die or go away. I can't emphasize enough how important this is. Even if you think that you've adequately reassured your child because you have said these words a hundred times, the likelihood is that you may need to say them a hundred times more before they become real for your child and truly comfort him.

• **Young children take comfort in daily routines.** In general, the more things change, the greater the sense of loss and grief. Simple things that structure a child's day—a morning stroll, a back rub before naptime, the evening bath, stories before bed—are a great source of comfort and reassurance. The days and weeks after a death are often very busy, so that daily routines tend to get pushed aside. If you can, try to stick to at least a few of these routines so your child has some stability amidst all the changes.

• **Children respond to the emotions around them.** Babies and toddlers are very sensitive to the emotions of the adults they rely on every day. A parent who is in the process of grieving can't hide this from a young child, and shouldn't try to. On the other hand, it may be frightening and confusing for a child to experience the full force of a parent's grief. Ideally, grieving parents can find ways to share their sad feelings with their children while staying in control. To do this, it helps if parents have adult friends and other support people to whom they can express the full extent of their sorrow.

• **Family strengths become more crucial in times of crisis.** There are many different sources of strength within families. Among these are close relatives, friends, traditions, and participation in religious and secular community organizations. Modern families often find themselves isolated, far from important relationships, too busy with hectic jobs to maintain the kinds of ties that could sustain them through trouble. Although it is never too late to rethink values and build a web of support, the best time is before a serious loss hits.

• **Grief takes time, but it is not forever.** After the immediate response to loss, adults often have to go through a long process of recovery before they are ready to move on in life. Old grief is never completely forgotten, but ideally it takes a position somewhere in the background, allowing life to go forward. There is no set time limit for this healing. For children, the process may be spread out over months or years, depending on the nature of the loss and the child's age. In general, the younger the child, the sooner you can expect a return to more or less normal activities. A toddler who has not been able to make this adjustment within three or four months may benefit from help from a professional. Seeking this help sooner rather than later makes great sense to me.

CHAPTER 4

Hygiene

*"Yes, bathing a baby or toddler can be
a bit of a messy and time-consuming chore at the
end of a busy day, but it does so much to put my
children and me in a great state of mind right
before their bedtime. They love the water and
their bath toys, and I love tucking them into
bed all clean and fresh smelling."*

—**StillLearning,** AS POSTED ON DRSPOCK.COM

Few things in the world smell sweeter than a baby—when she's smelling sweet, that is! There is no escaping the fact that young children are always getting dirty in some way or another. The daily round of diaper changes, face washing, and bathing can seem like a never-ending battle. On the other hand, these activities also give you a chance to have fun with your child, and do some teaching at the same time. Diaper changes and baths are good opportunities to teach your child the words for different body parts, for example. More important, the relaxed, pleasant way you go about doing these humble chores teaches your baby to enjoy her body and to feel good about her physical self. These early lessons help children to grow up emotionally healthy, as well as tidy. In this chapter, we'll explore everything from cutting a newborn's nails to dealing with bath-phobic toddlers. There will also be some "potty talk," as I explain all about diapering and toilet training.

Hygiene Basics

With babies, you have to relax your adult sense of hygiene, or you will drive yourself and your child crazy. On the other hand, a certain degree of cleanliness is important for health. The key to sensible hygiene is to accept a reasonable amount of dirt while keeping certain important areas clean. A good strategy is to create routines for everyday hygiene activities, such as diaper changes, baths, and general washing up. That way, your baby learns what to expect and it's easier for you to have everything you need right at hand.

While you are doing what you have to, it's important to keep some simple safety rules in mind. Actually, there are only two rules that are critical: Never leave a child alone on a changing table. It is amazing how quickly a baby can roll over the edge (even when he's supposedly too young for this maneuver). And never leave a baby or toddler alone in a baby bath or bathtub. Babies can drown in even a small amount of water, and in less time than you can imagine. I'll mention other safety tips later in the chapter, but these two are the most important by far.

Hygiene Issues at Different Ages

At first, your baby actually requires very little in the way of bathing, although you have to be diligent about not exposing him to too many germs. But soon your hygiene challenges will change, as your growing child begins to gleefully (and messily) discover the joys of mud pies, finger paints, solid foods, and everything else he can lay his hands on. Here are some pointers on keeping your child clean and healthy at various ages.

NEWBORNS

The best reason to pay special attention to a newborn's hygiene is to lower the risk of infections. One of the most important things you can do to ward off illness is to wash your own hands frequently. This is especially crucial if you've been preparing food or have been outside your home, activities that increase your exposure to germs you could pass along to your newborn. It's also a good idea to keep your baby away from people other than your immediate family as much as possible during the first two or three months of her life. This means staying out of crowds and not inviting a lot of friends and relatives to your home. A healthy adult, who is careful to wash her hands first, can safely hold

KEY: **N** =Newborn (0-2 mos.) **B** =Baby (2 mos.-1 yr.) **T** =Toddler (1-3 yrs.)

your newborn. But it's best if non-sibling children wait a couple of months to meet the newest member of your family. Older brothers and sisters, of course, need to touch their new babies. But they should always wash their hands first.

It takes a while for the immune system to kick in
To understand why all of these precautions make sense, you need to know something about your baby's immune system. During pregnancy, infection-fighting antibodies pass from the mother's bloodstream to her baby's. This wise arrangement ensures that when babies are born, they have some protection against many of the germs that they are likely to be exposed to as long as they stay close to their mothers. But they have much less protection against other germs (that is, germs that are new to their mothers). For example, if your sniffling seven-year-old nephew comes to visit, chances are good that his cold is something that your baby won't have much immunity against.

As they get older, babies begin to build up more of their own immunity, and they start to respond to minor infections more the way older children do. But while they are still in their first two or three months of life, they can become very ill with infections that wouldn't be any big deal later on.

A sponge bath is fine at first
New babies don't need tub baths. It's fine to simply take a soft, damp cloth and gently sponge off your baby. You'll need to clean the diaper area with each change, of

course. And you'll probably do some face wiping with each feeding. But the rest of your baby's body won't get that dirty. A sponge bath once a day, or every other day, is probably fine. Here are some tips to keep her first baths safe, easy, and fun:

• **A good place for a sponge bath is on a folded bath towel placed on the counter in your kitchen or bathroom.** It's safe, as long as you are right there to make sure your newborn doesn't fall off. The rule of thumb is always have at least one hand on your baby. You also can bathe your newborn in a tub or baby bath, but it's best to wait until the umbilical cord has fallen off so that the cord stump doesn't get soaked.

• **Have a soft, dry towel nearby so you can wrap your baby up snugly afterward.** Patting a baby dry, rather than rubbing, is gentler and just as effective.

• **You don't need to soap your baby all over.** For most body parts, warm water for washing and rinsing will do a fine job. The water should feel slightly warm—never hot!

• **You might want to use a little soap for the skin folds under your newborn's chin and arms, and between her legs.** Choose a gentle, moisturizing soap, free of coloring or scent. Soaps that advertise themselves as "pure" are often too harsh for a baby's skin, leaving it overly dry.

• **Go ahead and wash the soft spot on the top of your baby's head.** That area, called the fontanel, is covered by tough fibers under the skin. It only feels soft in comparison with the bones of the skull.

• **It's best not to put a cotton swab inside a baby's ears.** Just wash gently around the outside with a soft cloth, and use your finger to wipe around the opening to the ear canal. Any earwax will come out on its own. If you use a cotton swab, you'll only end up pushing the wax farther in.

• **For girls, gently spread the lips of the vulva and wash between them from front to back.** This helps ensure that remnants of bowel movements get pushed away from the vagina (otherwise they might increase the risk of a vaginal or bladder infection).

• **For uncircumcised boys, gently pull back the foreskin, but don't force it at all.** It's normal for foreskins in babies not to move. If you pull too hard, it will hurt, and there's a good chance that scar tissue will form between the foreskin and the head of the penis. For boys who have been circumcised, wash the head of the penis gently with a soft cloth, or just with water. Don't rub; it's bound to be tender. Once the circumcision has healed, you can wash the penis just like any other part of your baby.

• **Baby powder isn't usually necessary.** Powders that contain talc aren't safe for babies because they can cause lung irritation. Check the label. Cornstarch is safer, but it can be irritating, too, if a baby breathes in a big cloud of it. For a pudgy baby, powder can reduce rubbing between the skin folds. A little goes a long way, and if you put it on too heavily it will simply cake up or your baby will end up breathing it in.

Dry, peeling skin is normal right after birth
Most babies are born covered with a waxy substance called vernix. This protective coating comes off easily over the first couple of days with just normal wiping. Don't worry if your baby has dry, peeling skin. It usually takes a few days for the top few layers of dead cells to come off, exposing the fresh new skin underneath. There's no good way to rush the process.

Cradle cap is another very common, but not serious, problem. If you notice small, yellowish scales or flakes on your newborn's scalp, that's cradle cap. Most of the time, all you need to do is wash your baby's head using warm water and a soft cloth. If the flaking hasn't gone away after a couple of months, a mild dandruff shampoo containing selenium sulfide can often clear things up. For more severe or stubborn cases, there is also prescription medicine that can help.

Many newborns have rashes of one sort or another. Most of these are so common and minor that they are really normal. Pinhead-sized, pearly bumps over the nose and cheeks, called milia, are one of the more common, normal rashes. These go away over the first few months. Another rash carries the imposing name of erythema toxicum neonatorum. This refers to little reddish spots or bumps that appear at one or two days of age in almost half of healthy babies. The bumps go

Q: My two-month-old daughter has blocked tear ducts, which make her eyes run all the time. It's terrible! Sometimes she can't even open her eyes because they are caked over with green stuff. Will this ever get better?

A: While it's a nuisance, what you describe is very common and seldom causes a serious health problem. Here's what has happened: Normally, tears are cleared from the eye through tear ducts. When these ducts are blocked, the tears can build up and dry out, leaving clumps of yellowish discharge in the eye. Blocked tear ducts generally open up by themselves within the first few weeks or months of life. In rare cases, a minor surgical procedure is required to open them up. Sometimes gently massaging the ducts helps them open sooner, so ask your baby's healthcare provider if she thinks this is a good idea in your child's case.

In the meantime, the blockage can make your daughter more prone to eye infections, so be sure to clean her eyes very gently with a soft, clean, moist washcloth. If the amount of the discharge increases, or if the white parts of her eyes become red or swollen, it might mean that she has gotten an infection that requires an antibiotic ointment or drops, which her doctor can prescribe.

away by themselves a few days later. You don't have to do anything about this rash, despite its fancy name!

Other rashes, however, can be a sign of illness. Most of these illnesses are mild, but some are more serious. Be especially on the lookout for rashes that include blisters or pus-filled bumps; sometimes these are caused by bacteria or viruses that can spread through a baby's body. Rashes are hard to describe in writing. If you notice a rash and you're not sure that it's normal, it's best to talk with the doctor and have your baby examined.

The umbilical-cord stump requires extra care

You can relax about your baby's arms, legs, and face. But the umbilical cord is one area where cleanliness really does count. Soon after birth, the blood vessels leading to the umbilical cord clamp down, and the cord stump dies. It takes about two weeks for the stump to dry up and fall off. In the meantime, you need to keep the area clean and dry to prevent infection. The best advice about cord care is really just common sense:

• **Keep it as dry as possible.** It's OK for the stump to get wet, but it's best not to let it soak in water since it needs to dry out.

• **For the same reason, leave the cord area exposed to the air.** You may have to fold down the top of your baby's diaper, especially if you are using disposables, and roll up the bottom of his undershirt.

• **Gently wipe around the base of the stump using rubbing alcohol on a cotton swab or ball.** The alcohol won't sting your baby's skin, and the cord itself doesn't have any feeling at all. Doing this two or three times a day is usually enough to keep the area clean and speed up the drying process.

• **Don't worry about a slight odor or discharge.** As the cord gets ready to fall off, it might smell. You might even notice a small amount of fluid tinged with blood. This is normal, but you should clean the cord a bit more frequently with alcohol (as described above) so that it stays dry.

After the cord falls off, the base of your baby's bellybutton should dry up and heal within a few days. At that point, you can simply wash the area normally. Use a little soapy water on your finger, and then rinse the area well. You don't have to be nervous about pushing too hard; the skin at the base of the navel is just as strong as everywhere else on your baby's body.

If your baby's bellybutton stays moist or smelly even after the cord falls off, talk with your child's doctor. Usually the problem is caused by a patch of abnormal skin at the base of the navel called a granuloma. A doctor can paint on a chemical that causes the granuloma to dry up.

There is one serious problem that you should be aware of, even though it is rare. If the skin around your baby's cord becomes reddened, swollen, tender, warm, or firm, it could be a sign of a serious infection of the skin. If you notice any of these symptoms, be sure to have your baby seen by a doctor right away.

Fingernails and toenails need to be trimmed often

Babies' toenails and fingernails grow fast. Many newborns scratch their faces with their own fingernails as their little arms wave about. While this isn't a big problem, it's easy to prevent if you keep your baby's nails short and smooth. Nail clippers work, but you can't count on your baby's holding still, unless she is sleeping deeply. (The first time I clipped my own newborn's fingernails, I got a tiny bit of skin caught in the clipper and it bled. I felt terrible!) Biting a baby's nails often leaves jagged edges, so I don't recommend it.

A kinder, safer way is to use an emery board, the type you might use to shape and round your own nails. These small, flexible boards covered with sandpaper cannot hurt a baby's fingers, and they leave the nails smooth. If you shape your baby's nails two or three times a week, you may not ever have to clip them. Doing the nails this way takes a little longer, but the time can be well spent cuddling, talking, and playing "This Little Piggy" and other games. Instead of dreading clipping your baby's nails, you can look forward to the manicure as a special, fun activity.

OLDER INFANTS AND TODDLER

As babies move out of the newborn period, they develop new ways to get messy. Along with the joys of solid food come the challenges of oatmeal in the hair and bigger, smellier bowel movements. Once babies begin to crawl, they become magnets for any dust or dirt they encounter. Toddlers take joy in covering their hands, faces, and clothes with any substances they can find—finger paint, mud, or chocolate. On hot days, an active toddler may even develop mild body odor.

This is an age when children begin to develop life-long attitudes toward hygiene and habits. On the one hand, you want your child to value cleanliness. On the other hand, you don't want him to be so concerned with staying clean that he misses out on the fun of childhood. A well-adjusted toddler enjoys getting messy, and also enjoys getting cleaned up afterward.

Hand washing and tooth brushing

Your baby doesn't need to be spotless, but regular hand washing and tooth brushing are important for health. Get into the habit of washing your child's hands before and after each meal and snack. While your baby is still in the everything-goes-in-the-mouth stage, it's helpful to wash her hands several times during the day, as well.

Hand washing is especially important if you live in an older home. Buildings built before the 1970s all contain lead-based paint, either inside or on the exterior. As the paint ages, tiny bits flake off and become part of the house dust and the dirt around the house. If you think this might be a problem in your home, talk with your child's doctor or the health department.

Hand washing doesn't have to be a grim duty. Chat pleasantly or make up a hand-washing song. Find small bars of soap that your child can hold comfortably. Get a step stool so that she can reach the sink easily. By age two years, most toddlers can help with hand washing quite a bit. Praise your child for a job well done.

Good oral hygiene habits also are important to ingrain in your child. You can start brushing your baby's teeth as soon as the first one appears. Some parents begin even earlier, using a cloth to rub and clean the gums. A pea-sized dab of a fluoridated toothpaste is fine; any more, and your baby will simply end up swallowing it (see page 120 for more on fluoride in the diet).

If you start early, most babies accept tooth brushing as a normal part of the day. A few, however, resist with a passion. A firm, confident approach—"This is just something we have to do"—will help a balky or fearful baby accept the inevitable and eventually get used to it. It isn't important that you brush thoroughly or vigorously. But it is important that you succeed in brushing at least a little bit, so your child learns that making a fuss is not the way to go. (If, on the other hand, you feel yourself losing your temper, then it's wise to just stop. One day of unbrushed teeth won't do any real harm, and you'll be much more effective later when you're calm.)

Bath time
There are three main reasons to give your baby baths: to clean the areas that are soiled, to teach your baby how to take care of himself, and to have fun. All of these reasons are equally important, but busy parents sometimes forget about teaching and fun. That's too bad. Bath time is one of the very best events in the day

---

HYGIENE AND SAFETY 🏃

The most important hygiene consideration is, as always, safety. As infants and toddlers become more independent, they also face new hazards. They can crawl over to a cupboard and find a bottle of bleach, for example, or climb into the bathtub and turn on the hot water. It's wise to baby-proof your home as much as possible. You will want to install safety latches on any cupboard that contains a dangerous substance, such as bleach or toilet-bowl cleaner (or perhaps get rid of these substances altogether). You also may want to install a hook-and-eye latch on the bathroom door, high up out of your toddler's reach, so that he cannot get into the bathroom alone.

But even with the best baby-proofing, you still need to watch your infant or toddler all the time that he is up and about. The key safety rules are still the same: Never leave your young child unwatched in the bathtub, even for an instant. And never leave him alone on the changing table.

---

for you and your baby to enjoy each other. And chances are good that if you're both having fun, your baby is getting clean and learning at the same time.

As soon as the umbilical cord has dried up and fallen off—usually around the second or third week— it's safe to give your baby a tub bath as long as you are there the whole time. You can fill a tub with warm (not hot) water, and sit in it with your child on your lap. Or you can kneel or sit by the side of the tub. If you bathe your baby in the sink, you may want to put a towel in first, so he has something soft to sit on. You can also use a plastic baby bath. The ones with built-in foam pads may be more comfortable for your child.

There's no rule that says babies need a bath every day. But by four or five months, your baby may be messy enough that a daily bath makes sense, especially in hot weather or if he is roly-poly (dirt collects between those lovely rolls of skin, causing irritation). You can alternate tub baths and sponge baths, if you like.

Having a regular bath time (for example, after dinner) helps your baby know what to expect. Some babies are more flexible than others. How does your baby respond if his daily routine changes? Does he still eat and sleep well, and seem to enjoy himself? If you are lucky enough to have such a flexible baby, then sticking to a regular daily schedule may not be important. But if your baby gets thrown off by change, as many do, a regular routine of eating, sleeping, playing, and bathing will help him feel comfortable, and will make life easier for you as well.

Getting ready for the bath

The key to successful baby baths is to make sure you won't be interrupted and to have everything ready ahead of time. Your spouse or partner can answer the phone and take care of any other children. If you're by yourself, you can take the telephone off the hook or let the answering machine handle any calls. Your family and friends will soon learn not to try to call during bath time.

If you have everything ready ahead of time, you won't find yourself carrying around your wet baby while you go in search of a towel! If you realize you're missing the soap, the temptation to duck out of the room just for a second can be strong. But it takes only a second for a child to slip under the water. "Never leave a baby alone in the tub" should be an absolute rule. Among the things you'll probably want on hand are:

• **Soap.** A gentle moisturizing soap, without perfume or coloring, is usually best. Soap that is advertised as "pure" may be quite harsh. Whenever I see a baby with overly dry skin, I ask the parent if she's using so-called pure soap for the bath. Most of the time, I'm right!

• **Shampoo.** Any gentle shampoo will do. I don't believe that "no tears" shampoos really don't sting a baby's eyes, but they may not sting as much.

• **A washcloth.** And the softer, the better.

• **A plastic bucket or a plastic measuring cup for liquids.** Unless your tub has a spray nozzle on a hose, you'll need a clean bucket or cup for rinsing your baby's head and back.

• **Moisturizing cream or lotion.** This is especially important if your child has dry skin and during the winter months.

CLASSIC SPOCK
*"Most babies, after a few weeks'
experience, have a wonderful time
in the bath, so don't rush it. Enjoy it
with your baby."*

— Dr. Benjamin Spock, *Baby and Child Care*

• **Two big, soft towels.** One is for gently drying your baby and the other is just in case—you'd be surprised how much water a frolicking baby can displace. Hooded towels, while not necessary, are nice because they help keep a child warm while her hair is damp.

• **A few bath toys.** A very young baby is bound to be delighted with nothing more than water, you, and her own body to play with. But after age six or seven months, many babies enjoy watching things that float, splash, pour, or squirt. After 18 months or so, toddlers start using bath toys for make-believe. A couple of simple boats and a human figure or two can be used to tell any number of stories in the hands of an imaginative toddler.

Practical tips
• **Always test the water temperature before putting your child in the tub.** Babies have thin, delicate skin

that burns very easily. Use the back of your wrist or the inside of your elbow. The water should be warm, but not hot. If you use a bath thermometer, the temperature should not be over 100 degrees Fahrenheit.

• **If you can, adjust the temperature of your hot-water heater so that it heats only to 120 degrees.** Water feels hot at that temperature, but it takes several minutes to

---

ITEMS TO AVOID: BUBBLES AND 🏍 BATH RINGS

Although they're both quite popular, two products I recommend not using are bubble bath and bath rings or seats. Bubble-bath soap is often irritating to young children's eyes and skin. In particular, irritation to the very sensitive skin of a girl's vulva and outer vagina can cause a discharge, or itching. When girls rub or scratch, the irritation gets worse, which leads to even more scratching. It's probably best not to use bubble baths for babies and toddlers. And while bath rings or seats are designed to help babies sit up in the tub, they aren't safe. If they're using such a device, parents often are tempted to leave a baby alone in the tub for a little while. It's easy for babies to slip down under the water, or knock the ring over. Many babies drown each year because of these products.

---

scald a baby. At 130 degrees, a baby can be seriously burned before you realize what is happening. If you cannot turn down your water heater (because you live in an apartment, for example), there are safety devices you can buy that automatically stop the flow of water if it's hot enough to scald.

• **Put your baby in the tub while the water is filling.** That way, you won't ever lower your child into water that is too hot because you forgot to check.

• **Fill the tub only a few inches deep, so that it covers your baby's legs.** Your baby will be less likely to get a mouthful of water. But since babies can drown in just an inch or two of water, you still have to stay with your baby the whole time he is in the tub.

• **Use a towel or a foam pad under your baby for comfort.** And a padded rubber sleeve that fits over the spout can prevent injury if your active toddler bumps his head.

• **Once your child can crawl or walk, lock him out of the bathroom.** A simple hook-and-eye latch, high up on the door, will do the trick. A young child should never be alone in a bathroom.

Tub techniques
The bath shouldn't last more than about 10 minutes. Longer than that and the skin soaks up too much water and then becomes overly dry. (I'm not sure why being wet too long leads to overly dry skin, but it does.) If

227

your baby begins to look like a prune, she's probably been in the water too long.

Besides being vigilant about safety, there aren't any secrets to washing infants or toddlers. However, here are a few tips to keep in mind:

• When washing your baby's hair, tilt her face up, so that her hairline is actually below the level of her eyes. Then, when you pour water over her head, shampoo can't get into her eyes.

• Unless your baby is very dirty, try washing her face without soap. Plain water is gentlest, and usually does the trick.

• Concentrate on the folds of skin—under the arms, around the neck, between the legs—where grime accumulates and the skin rubs.

• Splash a little water into your child's ears to rinse out any extra wax. If you try to dig the wax out with a cotton swab, you're likely to end up pushing it farther into the ear canal. It's safe for children to get water in their ears, unless they have ear tubes in place or have a ruptured eardrum.

• You don't need to clean out your baby's nose, except to remove any dried mucus that's right at the opening.

• You can wash the bellybutton just like any other skin fold. It's not especially delicate.

• For girls, wash carefully between the skin folds of the vulva, washing from front to back, away from the opening of the vagina. Wash thoroughly, but don't scrub. Too much rubbing will cause irritation, which could result in itching or even discharge.

Fun and learning in the tub

Bath time, like other humble tasks such as diaper changing, is a learning opportunity for your child. Make a point of naming each body part as you wash it. Talk about what you're doing together (splashing, pouring, washing, and so on). Join your baby in tub play. If she wants to pour bathwater from a cup, let her pour and pour again. Each time she repeats the action, she is learning more. When she has learned all she needs to, she'll stop. If your child loves stories, you can find simple plastic books designed for the tub. Don't be surprised if she wants the same story over and over. Even though you are bored, she is picking up something new each time.

As your baby begins to show an interest in helping out with washing, let her. Praise her for being so capable. Eventually, you'll need to help only with the hard-to-reach spots. While you're cleaning your child's genital area, use the proper words for her parts: "Now we're washing your vulva [or "scrotum," for a boy]. We have to wash from front to back, so you'll stay healthy." Your matter-of-fact approach will tell your child that this is a part of the body that needs to be treated with respect (like the rest of the body), but not with fear, awe, or silence.

If you're not comfortable with the anatomical terms—penis and scrotum, vulva and vagina—it's fine to use less formal words. After all, very few children grow up knowing that their "tummy" is really their abdomen! But terms of avoidance such as "down there" and "your privates" give children the idea that there is something about their genitals that is mysterious, forbidden, possibly dangerous, and almost certainly exciting. In the long run, it's much healthier for children to develop a more realistic and matter-of-fact view of their sexual parts.

Bath time is also an opportunity for children to learn about limits. There are many things that young children can make decisions about—for example, how much they want to eat at dinner—but bath time is not one of those things. If your child hates baths, she still has to get clean. If your toddler loves the tub, she still has to get out after a reasonable amount of time. It's easy for bath time to become a battle of wills, with your toddler in tears and your nerves shot.

To help things run more smoothly, first try to see things from your child's point of view. If your child is busy playing, the bath may be an unwelcome interruption. Many young children have a very hard time shifting gears, moving from one activity to another. To help the transition go more smoothly, give your toddler plenty of advance notice: "It's time for your bath in five minutes. Get ready to stop and put things away." Give other announcements at three, two, and one minutes. If necessary, you can help your child begin to pick up and get ready to change activities.

Other toddlers resist the bath because their inborn temperament leads them to be physically sensitive and to reject change. The change in temperature, the wetness, the magnified bathroom sounds, and the smells of the bath could at first feel very uncomfortable to a sensitive toddler. Often, she might actually enjoy the bath after this response has worn off, but getting over the initial rejection can be a struggle. If you know that your child is likely to respond in this way, you can understand that she needs your support and encouragement to be able to wait for her body's negative reaction to pass.

The toddler who loves playing in the tub presents a different challenge. Give a two-minute, one-minute, and thirty-second warning to help your child move on to the next activity. Let her know that it isn't healthy to stay too long in the tub, and in matters of health and safety, there is no negotiation. While setting such a limit, it's OK to be sympathetic: "I know you just want to play a little longer, but we have to stop now. You can have another bath tomorrow." Your calm and kindly but firm limit-setting also teaches your child that you mean what you say, and that you will take action to make sure she is safe, even if she makes a fuss.

Diapering

Changing diapers is one of those things that non-parents have a hard time imagining. It's not just the mystery of how you can hold onto a squirming baby while wrapping a piece of cloth or plastic-covered paper around his bottom and pinning or taping it on. It's the idea that, several times a day, you can count on covering your hands with substances that you'd probably rather not even think about.

If you're a new parent, you'll probably be surprised at how readily you'll overcome any initial squeamishness. And believe it or not, sometimes it can even be fun. While some babies simply despise the whole process, many take delight in moving their legs freely and feeling the cool air on their bottoms. Babies are often wide-awake during diaper changes and in a social mood. While you're wiping up, it's easy to tickle your baby's tummy, "bicycle" his legs, or play patty-cake.

Like baths, diaper changes are a great time to talk with your baby. A natural thing to talk about while you're changing a diaper is your baby's body: arms, legs, tummy, toes, and also bottom and penis or vulva. Using the correct words for your baby's sexual parts makes sense, even though it is still many months until he starts talking. Parents of older children often fret about how to talk about sensitive subjects, such as where babies come from, and later, about love and sex. It's so much easier if relaxed conversation about the body is simply a natural part of what you do as a family, right from the beginning.

CLOTH OR DISPOSABLE DIAPERS?

Assuming that your baby goes through 10 diapers a day—the actual number depends on your baby's size, age, diet, and habits—you'll need about 70 diapers a week. In an average month, that comes to about 300 diapers, or roughly 3,600 diapers over your baby's first year. That's a lot of diapers!

You can certainly find parents and other experts who feel strongly that one kind of diaper—cloth or disposable—is better than the other. By far, most parents in the United States end up using disposables. But what's best for others may not be what's best for your baby and you. For many families, a combination of cloth and disposables works well. Here are some factors to consider.

Cost

The least expensive option is to buy cloth diapers and launder them yourself. The diapers sell for between $1.50 and $5 apiece, and you'll want about three dozen of them (total cost, between $50 and $180). When you add in the cost of diaper covers, laundry detergent, and hot water, the total is about $300 to $800 per year. There are mail-order stores that sell every conceivable variety of cloth diaper, from the kind that is nothing more than a rectangle of absorbent cotton to high-tech varieties with elastic, snaps and tabs, breathable outer covers, and special pockets to hold the absorbing material. The fancier you get, the more you pay.

Paying a diaper service to deliver clean diapers once or twice a week saves you from having to do all that laundry. Diaper services cost about $600 to $900 per year, depending on where you live, how many diapers you order, and what kind of diaper covers you choose. Some services require you to buy the diapers yourself; others provide them. A diaper pail often comes with the deal.

The cost of disposable diapers is similar to the cost of a diaper service, about $600 to $900 per year. You can save some money by using coupons, looking for sales, buying in bulk, and avoiding the big-name brands. Still, there is a hidden cost to disposables, as well. They are quite expensive to get rid of. The solid-waste disposal costs are usually borne by governments, so the costs show up in our taxes. Some municipalities actually pay parents to use cloth diapers because it's cheaper than dealing with dirty diapers in the trash stream.

Convenience

Most parents feel that disposables win for convenience, hands down. Disposables are easier to put on than old-fashioned diapers that require pinning (however, many modern cloth diapers use Velcro fasteners instead). They seem to leak less than cloth diapers, although I suspect that many cloth supporters would disagree. They may be especially useful for nighttime, when changes are less frequent, and leakage can mean that you have to wash pajamas, sheets, blankets, and mattress covers.

Disposables are clearly more convenient when you're traveling. It's much easier to toss out a wrapped-up disposable than to have to carry around soiled cloth diapers and find a place to wash them. It makes sense to have a few disposables around for this purpose, unless you are strongly opposed to them for environmental or health reasons.

❝

PARENT TO PARENT
"My son is a wriggler and I don't even use his changing table for fear of his launching off. I sit on the floor with my legs in a 'V.' I put him in between my legs and close them on each side of him so he is restrained from moving side to side. Then I make faces and he usually is complacent."

— **kkcarrino,** AS POSTED ON DRSPOCK.COM

Obviously, you don't have to wash disposable diapers. But you shouldn't just wrap them up and toss them out, either. First, you need to dump any solid waste into the toilet to keep human waste out of landfills as much as possible. (In many places, it's illegal to dump human waste into landfills, although I've never heard of this law's being enforced when it comes to diapers.)

There are other hassles with disposables, as well. You have to lug them home from the store, and, for some reason, you always seem to run out of them at the least convenient times possible, like the middle of the night. You also have to take out the trash frequently or it smells awful, no matter how many deodorizing disks you stick in your diaper pail.

With cloth diapers, you have to plan on changing them more often—which is probably better for your baby in any case. If you use a diaper service, you need to set the dirty ones out for pick-up, and carry the clean ones inside. If you are doing your own laundering, you should count on doing three or four more loads of wash a week. Many parents find they need to run diapers through the rinse cycle twice or their babies develop rashes.

Effectiveness

Disposable diapers do absorb more urine than cloth, but if you change a cloth diaper frequently, it works just as well. Compared with disposable diapers, which have plastic outer shells, cloth diapers allow some air circulation, which helps keep the skin dry. On the other hand, cloth diapers may be more prone to leaking. Plastic outer pants cut down on leakage, but also eliminate any airflow.

Leakage is a special issue for children in daycare settings, where the risk of passing infections from child to child is quite high. Some centers discourage parents from using cloth diapers.

For cloth users, there are several ways you can improve the diapers' effectiveness. You can double-diaper, or use a special "diaper doubler," a smaller piece of absorbent cloth that fits inside the regular diaper. For boys, a diaper doubler does most good in the front; for girls, in back. You also can buy inexpensive diaper liners, which are sheets of disposable material that let urine through, but keep stool from getting onto the diaper itself. Liners create space between your baby's bottom and the diaper, which helps with airflow and dryness. And you can simply flush them down the toilet, along with whatever's in them.

Environmental impact

Disposable diapers require a great deal of wood pulp, petroleum, and energy to produce and package. Even more important, they take up space in landfills—around 3 percent of all landfill space, by most estimates. That may not sound like much except when you consider that diapers are only one product out of many thousands and they are only used by babies, who make up a small segment of the overall population. And they contain plastic, which is very slow to decompose (this is true even of newer so-called biodegradable plastic).

Cloth diapers also have an environmental impact. They take energy and water to clean and dry. Many commercial diaper services use strong detergent and chlorine bleach to keep from spreading infections, and the contaminated rinse water is a pollutant. If you use a diaper service, you have to factor in the air pollution and fuel expenditures by the delivery trucks.

So which type is really better for the earth? The question of the relative environmental impacts of cloth and disposable diapers caused a big flurry a few years ago. After environmental groups pointed out the toll of disposables, diaper manufacturers responded with their own study that claimed that the environmental impacts of disposables and reusables were about equal. There are experts on both sides of the debate.

237

Health concerns

Diaper rashes bother most babies at least some of the time. Mild diaper rashes are uncomfortable, but not dangerous. Still, diaper rashes can grow into serious skin infections, so it's best to prevent them if possible. Several studies show that disposable diapers are better at preventing diaper rashes. However, you have to be a bit skeptical, since many of these studies were paid for by diaper manufacturers. With frequent changes, I think cloth diapers can work just as well, if not better.

Most disposables contain a chemical that holds water in the form of a gel. The gel, a whitish substance that looks like salt when it's dry, sometimes leaks out. There is no evidence that it is dangerous to children, although some children may be sensitive to it or other chemicals used in the manufacturing process. If your child develops a rash, one possibility is that it is a reaction to chemicals in the diaper itself.

There is some reason to be concerned about a completely different health issue that affects only boys. Because disposable diapers seal tighter and allow less air circulation, they result in higher skin temperatures. This is important because it means that the scrotum, and the testicles within the scrotum, are warmer. And testicles need to be relatively cool to function normally. Although baby boys are years away from sexual maturity, their testicles are busy making sperm cells. So, the concern is that perhaps the warmer testicle temperatures, caused by disposable diapers, will result in lowered fertility years down the road. This concern makes sense to me. But it is still only a theory.

OTHER DIAPERING EQUIPMENT

Once you've gotten past the cloth-versus-disposable dilemma, the rest of your diapering decisions should be easy. You'll need a convenient and hygienic place to do the changing, wipes and ointment for your baby's bottom, and somewhere to toss the dirties. A well-made diaper bag also is a must.

Changing tables are a practical luxury
Although it is a staple in many nurseries, you don't really need a changing table. You can change your baby on a bed, or on a towel or pad on the floor. Either of these is likely to be hard on your back, though. A well-made changing table holds the baby up high, is sturdy, and has a padded surface, rails or sides around the top, and a safety strap. Storage space for diapers, diaper covers, wipes, and ointment is a plus. A table that converts into a dresser can save money in the long run, after your diapering days are over.

Wipes should be soft, strong, and free of irritants
What you want in a wipe is softness and strength. Pre-moistened wipes save a little time. To save money, you can make your own by cutting up some soft paper towels and pouring water over them. Beware of wipes that have alcohol, perfume, or other chemicals that can irritate your child's skin. Some wipes have aloe or other herbal ingredients; they probably don't do any good or any harm. An electric wipe warmer (about $20) is a nice gizmo, but not a necessity.

Ointments help protect a baby's skin

A good ointment really does help protect your baby's bottom. Regular petroleum jelly (Vaseline and other brands) is cheap and effective. Ointment with zinc oxide works well, too. Ointments are petroleum-jelly based. They create a waterproof covering for your baby's bottom. Creams are oil and water based. They don't work as well as ointments because they let more water through and urine washes them right off. If your child's bottom is rash free, a little baby oil at diaper changes might be all you need to keep it that way.

Diaper pails help confine the mess

There is no such thing as a diaper pail that is truly odor free, unless it's never been used. Many come with deodorizers, which give off their own peculiar smell. For cloth diapers that you wash yourself, fill your diaper pail about halfway with water. Adding a quarter cup of bleach or vinegar, or a tablespoon or two of borax, can cut down on staining and odors. Be sure that the lid fits tightly and that the pail is beyond the reach of any crawling babies or toddlers. Otherwise, there is a real drowning risk. If you use bleach, be careful to store it safely, as well. Children can easily mistake white bleach bottles for milk, and many have suffered serious injuries to the mouth and throat from drinking bleach.

A nifty invention called a "Diaper Genie" can make it easier to get rid of dirty disposables by sealing them in plastic that locks away germs and odors. These units cost $25 to $35, and you have to buy special refill bags for another $10 to $15 per month. Keep in mind, though, that diapers treated in this way will take even longer to break down in landfills.

For diaper services, you can often just toss the diaper, poop and all, into the pail supplied by the service. With disposable diapers, you have to empty any solid waste into the toilet, then wrap the diapers up in themselves and toss in the garbage. If you forget to empty the garbage every couple of days, the smell is bound to remind you.

Diaper bags are a must

A good diaper bag has lots of space, sturdy handles, and washable surfaces. You'll need to stock it with diapers, diaper wraps (those nifty, pinless, breathable-but-waterproof covers for cloth diapers), a plastic bag for the dirties, pre-moistened wipes, ointment, and towels for drying and to wipe up any mess. It also should have space for a changing pad to cushion your baby while she's being changed; many bags these days have built-in pads that are easy to wash. It's also a good idea to carry a change of clothes or two, as well as snacks and formula (unless you are nursing, of course). You'll also want to carry a few special toys, in case your baby gets bored. A shoulder strap frees up your hands.

DIAPERING TECHNIQUES

By giving these tips, I don't mean to suggest that there is anything difficult about diapering. In fact, diapering is easy. I feel that it's important to state this up front, so that no father gets the idea that he can escape by pleading incompetence. Fathers can diaper, even (or especially!) half asleep in the middle of the night. That said, there are just a few tips and techniques to keep in mind:

• **When and how often should you change a diaper?** A good time is soon after your baby has eaten. Babies tend to move their bowels when they fill up their stomachs (doctors call this the gastro-colic reflex). The best time to change a diaper is as soon as you can, once you know it's wet or soiled. With super-absorbent disposables it can be hard to tell. If the diaper starts sagging with the weight of the urine it contains, it's probably past due for a change.

• **Keep your baby safe.** Each year, there are some 3,000 injuries reported when babies fall from their changing tables. That's a pretty alarming number. A good rule of thumb is to never walk away and leave your baby on the changing table. Instead, if you have to answer the phone, pick him up and take him with you. If your table has a safety strap, use it. But don't count on it's keeping your baby from falling off.

• **Have everything ready.** There's nothing quite like taking off your baby's diaper, realizing that he is completely covered in poop, and then realizing that the diaper wipes are in the other room. This happens to every parent at least once, I am convinced. After that, we learn to be prepared.

• **Keep pins sharp.** If you're using traditional cloth diapers, make sure that your diaper pins are sharp. If you have to push too hard because the pin is dull, you're more likely to slip and poke somebody (guess who?). Storing safety pins by sticking them into a bar of soap is a good trick. That way, they slip through the fabric more easily. Get rid of old pins with cracked plastic heads; they're not safe.

• **Clean your baby thoroughly**. For girls, gently wipe between all the skin folds, allowing water to run down between the labia to clean the entrance to the vagina. Wipe from front to back, to lower the risk of vaginal and bladder infections. For boys, as soon as you take the diaper off, be ready in case your baby decides to pee—many a parent has been surprised by the little yellow fountain! While you clean your baby's bottom, keep a diaper or wipe over his penis, so you won't get sprayed. If he is not circumcised, drip water over the tip of the penis and gently wipe away any dirt or old skin cells. Don't try to pull the foreskin back with any force. It will pull back easily later, usually in a year or two. For both sexes, if the babies are very soiled, a quick bath might be in order to really get their bottoms clean.

• **Take the time to dry.** Use a soft cloth, and pat, don't rub. Rubbing causes tiny scratches in the skin that let acid and germs in, opening the way for diaper rashes. Once the skin is dry, apply any good ointment (see page 240 for hints) to keep moisture away.

• **Give your baby a little "air time" each day.** Every baby I've met loves the feeling of going diaperless. And a baby's bottom is never as dry in a diaper as it is out in the open. Lay your young baby on a soft towel over a linoleum or wooden floor, or on top of a thick plastic sheet on top of the carpet. (Remember, thin plastic like that found in plastic bags or kitchen wrap poses a suffocation risk.) By 12 to 15 months, many babies have enough control to hold their urine for several minutes at a time. Knowing that the diaper goes back on at the first sign of urination is a strong incentive for toddlers to keep control. If the weather's nice, let your toddler enjoy the great outdoors with nothing on below (except perhaps sunscreen).

• **Get a good fit.** With disposable diapers, there's very little challenge. Even if you put them on backwards, they still work pretty well! (Hint: The colorful waistband usually goes in front.) With cloth, the best way is to have someone with experience show you how to diaper a couple of times, then experiment on your own. Fold traditional flat diapers lengthwise in thirds, then spread the top and bottom of the folds out, to reach around your baby's hips. When pinning, slip a finger between the diaper and your baby, so your baby won't get poked.

• **Be sure to wash up.** After every diaper change, be sure to wash your own hands thoroughly. Good hand washing is always the most effective means of preventing infections.

Diapering a squirmy baby

There are some babies who are happy to lie still for diapering. If you're lucky enough to have one of these easy-to-diaper babies, you can skip this section. But lots of babies are anything but easy. They squirm, wriggle, and roll over, or insist on standing up. When you try to hold them down, they struggle and howl with anger. These babies, believe it or not, often grow up to be perfectly calm, well-mannered children and adults. So you don't need to worry that they'll always be "hyper" or uncontrollable; you just need to get through the diapering stage without losing your patience—or losing your baby over the side of the changing table. Here are some tips to help you:

• Have everything ready ahead of time: diapers, wipes (open the box), ointment (unscrew the cap), a cloth for drying, and if you are using cloth diapers, pins or a diaper cover.

• If you're using cloth, have the diaper pinned already, and slip it on over your baby's legs, like pants. Or use a diaper cover with Velcro or snap closings.

• Hang an interesting mobile above the changing table (but well out of your baby's reach). Reserve an attractive rattle or other engaging toy as a special diaper-time-only diversion.

• Sing, talk to your baby, or play music that your baby really likes—anything to capture his attention!

245

• Make the diapering part of a simple and silly game, such as "Where's your tummy? There's your tummy." Babies can't laugh with delight and howl with indignation at the same time.

• Get help from another adult or an older child if you can. A four-year-old can help distract the baby; a six-year-old can help keep him from rolling over while you concentrate on getting the diaper on.

• If your baby insists on standing up, let him! With a little practice, it's possible to slip a diaper on a child standing, or even lying on his tummy.

Washing diapers and soiled clothing
Whether you use disposables or cloth, there's no way to completely avoid wet and soiled clothing, sheets, blankets, and towels. With diapers, it's a good idea to rinse them ahead of time (the toilet works well for this), and wash them separately from other laundry.

• Use hot water, to kill more germs.

• Use a laundry detergent without a lot of perfumes. If you use a powder, make sure it dissolves completely, so that it rinses out fully.

• Add a cup of chlorine bleach or a couple of tablespoons of borax to the wash to combat germs. (Remember, however, that some babies may be sensitive to bleach, so watch for signs of skin irritation.)

• Make sure everything is rinsed well. Even a little soap left in a diaper or undershirt can irritate a baby's skin. Many parents end up rinsing baby clothes two or three times.

• You can add a half cup of white vinegar to the last rinse to soften diapers and underclothes and to make them more absorbent. Don't use fabric softeners, because they can irritate a baby's skin; they also make cloth less absorbent.

• Dry diapers, clothes, and bedclothes using high heat or in the sun. Don't let them sit around damp; that encourages mold to grow.

DIAPER RASHES

No matter how careful you are about diapering, chances are your baby will have a diaper rash at least once. There are many causes for rashes in the diaper area. But you need to know about only a few common ones to be able to handle diaper rashes most of the time.

Irritant rashes
This is what most people mean when they talk about diaper rash: red, tender skin on the buttocks and inner thighs, caused by irritation from urine and stool, as well as friction between the skin and diaper. The rash is usually worse on areas of skin that are exposed. If you look inside the folds of skin on your baby's thighs and

247

between the buttocks, you normally won't find a rash because these areas are less exposed to urine. The best way to prevent and treat this problem is frequent diaper changes and air time, as described earlier. Petroleum jelly or zinc oxide ointment helps protect the skin so it isn't irritated further. I don't know of any medicine that specifically treats this rash, however. The skin just needs time to heal.

If you notice a rash right after changing to a new brand of disposable diaper, or after using a new detergent or fabric softener, the rash might be due to a mild reaction to chemical irritants. Changing back to the old diapers, double or triple rinsing, or not using fabric softener may be the solution.

Rashes with diarrhea
Diarrhea is very acidic and irritating. You'll find the rash caused by diarrhea in the same areas as the usual diaper rash, but also between the buttocks and concentrated around the anus. If it's severe, there can be a little bleeding. The treatment is the same as for a common irritant rash, along with whatever treatment the doctor recommends for the diarrhea itself. In bottle-fed children, a bit of irritation right around the anus is pretty common, even without diarrhea. It usually goes away once solid foods make up more of their diet.

Yeast infections
If a diaper rash doesn't get better with the normal treatment, your baby could have a yeast infection, also called *Candida* or *Monilia* infections. Diaper rashes caused by

yeast have a particular appearance. They are usually a deep red, beefy color. They have a sharp border, unlike irritant diaper rashes, which fade into the surrounding skin. There are often little round, red sores surrounding the large central red area. The rash is often worse on the inside of the thighs and inside skin folds, where the skin is especially moist.

Yeast infections are more likely if your baby has just taken antibiotics. Antibiotics kill harmful bacteria, but they also kill the good bacteria that normally live in the intestines. Once these helpful bacteria are dead, the yeast are free to multiply like mad, causing an infection. Thrush is an infection in the mouth caused by the same yeast that cause *Candida* diaper rashes. In the mouth, thrush looks like little patches of curdled milk that don't wash or rub off easily (see page 165). If your baby has a deep red diaper rash and thrush, chances are good that yeast are behind both infections.

Yeast infections are very uncomfortable for babies, but they aren't dangerous and they are usually easy to treat. Typically, a doctor will prescribe an antifungal medicine, such as nystatin. It comes in an ointment for the bottom and in a liquid for the mouth. You also need to keep your baby's bottom dry and clean, with frequent diaper changes and as much air time as possible.

Blisters and other rashes
Skin infections can cause rashes in the diaper area with blisters or crusts. The blisters can be filled with clear or cloudy fluid. The crusts can be deep red, black, or honey colored. These rashes need to be seen by a doctor and

249

treated promptly, or they can spread and become very serious. A good rule of thumb is, if your baby has a diaper rash that is not clearly due to irritation (as described above), you should have him checked by his doctor to be sure no infection is present.

Diapering and sexual health

Diaper changing brings up issues that make many parents uncomfortable. You're cleaning up your baby boy and he gets an erection. Or as soon as the diaper is off, your daughter's hands make their way to her vulva. These behaviors may suggest adultlike sexual responses, but they are really very different. Unlike adults, babies don't give any special meaning to the sensations that arise in their genitals. Erections are not signs of sexual excitement, but are reflex responses to changes in temperature or friction, bladder fullness, or other internal sensations. Genital touching by a baby does not have the same meaning as masturbation by an adolescent, because babies don't have sexual fantasies. The genitals are just parts of the body that are pleasant to touch, like the earlobes, knees, and toes.

Even though your baby's genital exploration is not sexual in the adult sense, diaper changes do give you an opportunity to communicate some of your values to your baby. If you tell your daughter "No!" whenever you notice her rubbing or touching her vulva, you communicate that there is something bad, wrong, or perhaps dangerous about that part of the body. If you snatch her hands away, and rush to cover up the offending area, you send the same message.

On the other hand, if you make a neutral comment, such as "I see you like to touch your vulva," and go about the business of the diaper change, you communicate that it's OK to talk about the genitals. As your child grows, questions about genitals and sexuality are bound to arise many times. By making it clear from the start that you are comfortable talking about these issues, you make it easier for your child to come to you with questions and concerns. And with each conversation, you have the chance to convey your personal values about sexuality. Not talking about these issues doesn't make your child's questions or concerns go away; it only means that you may not have a chance to help your child deal with them.

Toilet Training

When you think about toilet training, do you see the light at the end of the tunnel, or do you see only the tunnel? The good news about toilet training is that many toddlers master the potty easily and are proud of their accomplishment. The bad news is, toilet training can be a long and frustrating ordeal. Everyone knows of children who refuse to give up their diapers, or who use their potties for everything except what they're made for.

It doesn't help that there is no single "right" method. If you've listened to family members, your child's doctor, and the experts who write books, you've probably heard plenty of conflicting advice. It can be hard to sort through it all to find the parts that make sense to you.

I'll try to help. In the sections that follow, I present several different approaches to toilet training, talking about advantages, disadvantages, and pitfalls. Every method works some of the time, and no method that I know of works all of the time. The important thing is for you to decide on an approach that fits you and your child. Chances are, if you feel good about your choice and it makes sense to you, you'll be successful at toilet training.

Before we start, though, a word about words: In order to toilet train your child, you need to be able to talk about what's happening using friendly-sounding terms. "Urinate" and "defecate" are simply too long and hard for a child to understand and pronounce. In the sections that follow, I'll use "pee," "poop," and "BM"

PARENT TO PARENT
"Don't get confused by parents who brag about how easy and fast their child got potty trained—every child is different. In general, girls are said to be easier than boys, but that wasn't the case with my kids. Just be patient and hang in there and it will happen."

—**jensmom,** AS POSTED ON DRSPOCK.COM

(bowel movement), but it doesn't matter what words you choose, as long as you're comfortable saying them.

TRAINING BY REFLEX

During the early 20th century in the United States, babies were toilet trained by reflex. According to the experts of the time, mothers were to take their babies to the toilet several times a day, all strictly scheduled, and stimulate them to defecate. The response would become a conditioned reflex, like teaching a dog to salivate when a bell is rung.

A less rigid method of reflex training, more responsive to the baby, is traditional in many parts of the world today. Starting in the first months of life, whenever a mother senses her baby has to go, she carries him over to the potty and tries to catch the urine or BM. At the same time, she makes a "psssss" sound. After a while, she begins taking him to the potty several times a day, especially after meals, when a bowel movement is most likely. She makes the sound, and waits for the baby to produce. When he does, she praises him.

To understand how these methods work, it helps to know about reflexes. In order to pee, the muscle of the bladder has to contract while other muscles that block the flow of urine relax. For pooping, a similar process has to take place, with one set of muscles squeezing while another set lets go. These muscles are controlled by automatic reflexes. There are other muscles that are under conscious control. We all become very aware of them when we feel the urge but can't get to the bathroom right away.

The process of training relies on building a connection in the baby's brain between the potty, the presence of the mother, the special sound, and the act of peeing or pooping. Whenever the first three of these features are present (potty, mom, and the special sound), the fourth soon follows. After many repetitions, the baby's reflexes become trained so that the act of taking him to the potty and making the sound brings about the reflex squeezing of the bladder and rectum. In this way, a baby can be successfully out of diapers as early as 12 or 15 months.

Advantages and disadvantages

The obvious advantage of this approach is that you can say goodbye to diapers sooner. A disadvantage is that it takes a great deal of effort early on. You need to be at home with your baby nearly all of the time, so that the potty is never far away. Many of the distractions of modern life—such as going to the grocery store—would interfere. A baby trained by reflex remains dependent on you (or another caring adult) for frequent trips to the potty.

Another disadvantage is that the training may not last. If you get very good at catching your baby in the act of having a BM, you may think that you have her trained well before her first birthday. However, once she starts moving around more and her bowel movements become less predictable, the training vanishes. Compared with the approach described below, the chance of having a problem with wetting later on may be greater.

SIT! STAY! PEE!

This is what many parents think of as toilet training. You wait until your child is walking well, about 15 or 16 months old. Then, several times a day, when you suspect that he may have to pee, you walk him to the bathroom, take off his diaper and put him on the toilet. There he stays until he produces or some period of time has gone by (say 15 minutes)—or until he has a tantrum. Your job, as parent, is to keep him on the toilet.

A variation of this approach is the "just get rid of the diapers" strategy. You start by buying a pair of special underpants for your child, decorated with his favorite cartoon character. When you decide he is ready, you announce that he is now old enough for "big-boy pants." You swap the special underpants for the diaper, and tell your child that he needs to start using the potty or the toilet. Then you remind him several times a day to "go and try to pee." When you think he might have to go, you walk him to the bathroom and sit him on the potty. You wait for results, and praise him if he happens to pee while sitting.

Advantages and disadvantages
These approaches work best for parents who are very patient and persistent, and for children who are very

willing to please their parents and able to sit long enough to succeed. Often, however, the result is far less positive. The child may resent being whisked away from whatever fun activity he was engaged in to go sit on the toilet for what seems like an eternity. He may have no real idea of what he's supposed to do, or how to do it. In these instances, both parent and child are likely to become frustrated. After wetting his special underpants several times and being scolded for it (or simply feeling that he has let his parents down), the child is likely to decide that diapers are, on the whole, safer. Sometimes this leads to a potty boycott that lasts for months.

Parents who are less patient are apt to try to speed things up by scolding or punishing their child for "accidents." For example, they threaten to take away the great new underpants and put their child back in diapers "like a baby." This strategy almost always fails. Punishment can teach a child that wetting is bad, but it can't teach him how to stay dry. The first step in voiding is to relax the pelvic muscles. When a child's time on the potty is stressful, it can be difficult or even impossible for him to let go. The longer he sits, the tenser he gets. Then, when he finally gets up from the potty, he's so relieved to be free that his whole body relaxes, and he pees or poops in his underpants or diaper. From the parent's point of view, the child is simply being stubborn or spiteful, intentionally waiting until he is off the potty to go. It's easy to see how ineffective toilet training can lead to anger and unhappiness, and even to child abuse in rare cases.

A CHILD-CENTERED APPROACH

Forty years ago, Dr. T. Berry Brazelton, the renowned American pediatrician, realized that children could learn to use the toilet without being forced, scolded, or punished. If parents waited until their children were developmentally and emotionally ready, then let the children set the pace, most of the children succeeded at a reasonable age, with little frustration and few incidents of backsliding or other problems. This innovative and sensible approach, which Dr. Brazelton called child-centered, is now accepted by most pediatricians and family doctors as the best way to go about toilet training.

The key is to start the toilet-training program only once your child is developmentally ready. This is usually between 20 and 30 months, but it is later for some children and earlier for a few. Signs that your child is ready include:

• Your child can walk over to the potty, and sit on it securely. She can help slip down her pants and diaper.

• Your child has begun to notice the feeling of fullness in the bladder or rectum that means it's time to "go," and she can tell you with words or signs.

• Your child's diapers are dry between changes a couple of times a day or more (a sign of bladder maturity).

• Your toddler takes a keen interest in what you, or an older sibling, do in the bathroom.

257

• Your toddler is able, at least some of the time, to cooperate when you ask her to do something, like get her shoes. She may show a new interest in putting things—toys, clothes—in their proper places.

• She also shows a new interest in the plastic potty you bought months ago, which has been sitting unnoticed in a corner of the living room.

The training itself follows this plan: Around 18 months, you purchase a plastic potty and let your child know that it is her own special chair. At the same time, if not before, you allow your toddler to come with you when you go to the bathroom, to watch what you do. You encourage your toddler to sit on the potty, fully clothed, and reward her with praise and a story, or a cookie, when she does. You explain that the toilet and the potty are for the same purpose. If your child resists sitting on the potty, don't force the issue. She's free to come and go as she pleases.

After your child has been sitting on the potty fully clothed for a week or so, you encourage her to sit there without her diaper on (being without a diaper is usually a treat for a toddler!). But don't try to get her to produce. Once she's quite comfortable sitting on her special seat, you take her there when she has a full diaper and show her that the potty is made to hold the pee and poop. Again, you wait until your child is comfortable with the idea. Only then do you encourage her to sit on the potty when she needs to go. Finally, when she does pee or poop in the potty, you praise her for being "grown up," being careful to not make too big a deal of it. Toddlers like to feel they are following their own will, not giving in to their parents' wishes.

After your toddler has managed to pee in the potty, you can take her over several times during the day to catch her pee or poop. After a week or more, when she's happily going with you to the potty, you can let her go for blocks of time without a diaper on, perhaps in loose-fitting underpants that are easy to take up and down. Encourage her to use the potty herself when she needs to. You may need to remind her a bit, but you don't push her to use the potty, or criticize her for any accidents. At this point, most children are very proud of their ability to go all by themselves.

Throughout the process, you encourage your child but move forward at her pace. There's no set time schedule. If you feel your child resisting, it's wise to drop the issue for a few weeks or even months. Especially between 12 and 18 months, toddlers often develop a fondness for their bowel movements and a reluctance to see them whisked away. If they see that you are dead set on controlling where and when they go, they are bound to resist. After about 18 months, these impulses taper off a bit, and children are ready to move ahead with toileting again.

Advantages and disadvantages

Children who learn to take control of their toileting gain more than just dry bottoms. They feel proud of their new accomplishment. They have learned how to hold on when they need to, and let go when they want to. By earning the right to wear "big-kid" underwear, they have taken a giant step toward independence.

The evidence that this child-centered approach is highly effective comes primarily from Dr. Brazelton's own research. Out of 1,170 children whose parents were taught the approach, 80 percent were successfully out of diapers during the day between two and two-and-a-half years of age, and most (again, 80 percent) were dry at night by age three. By age five, very few children (less than 2 percent) developed constipation, bedwetting, or other toileting problems, well below the national average.

More recently, however, another pediatrician has reported that about one-fifth of children in his practice who were trained using a low-pressure, child-centered approach developed a problem he calls "stool toileting refusal." This is when children use the potty to urinate, but insist on having their diaper on to have a bowel movement. This behavior often drives parents crazy. Children with this problem tend to toilet train later, but otherwise they are not very different from other children.

I suspect that some children are simply not very interested in giving up their diapers. Their parents, following the standard advice, wait and wait for their children to take the initiative. After a while, when nothing much has happened, the parents start reminding or nudging. If the child then digs in her heels, a frustrating standoff can follow. Usually, the problem goes away on its own. In other cases, the solution is for parents to stop all pressure to perform and simply put their children back in diapers. Within a few weeks to months, most children decide to accept the potty.

Perhaps the biggest problem with the advice to "go at your child's pace" is that, for many parents, that pace simply isn't fast enough. And there are good reasons why you might need your child out of diapers sooner rather than later. You may worry that your toddler will not be welcomed in a child-care center in diapers (although, of course, centers that care for infants accept diaper changing as part of the job). If you use a babysitter or home child-care provider, you may feel pressure from those helpers to get the diaper phase over with. Or you may be expecting another child and don't relish changing two sets of diapers in the midst of all your other duties.

A TEACHING APPROACH

You can teach your toddler to use the potty independently, without scolding or punishing, and also without having to wait for him to take the lead. The key to making this work is to wait until he is ready (as with the child-centered approach), and then to use a whole collection of effective teaching methods, all at once.

A good description of this approach appeared in the 1970s in a book called *Toilet Training in Less Than a Day* by Nathan Azrin and Richard Foxx. The authors, both experienced psychologists, laid out a step-by-step teaching plan through which a toddler can learn to use the potty on his own and empty it into the toilet.

Despite the book's catchy title, the whole teaching process takes longer than one day, although the core training does take only a few hours—much faster than the child-centered approach described above. After that, there is follow-up teaching to help the child solidify his new skills.

The book describes the teaching program in great detail. I'll try to give you a flavor of it here, but if you want to use this method, you should purchase the book (it's not expensive), and read it carefully.

Before beginning the actual training, you need to make sure that your child is ready. Usually, this will not be before 20 months, about the same age you might start using the child-centered approach. The signs of readiness are like those for the child-centered approach. Azrin and Foxx present these signs in three simple tests:

• **Bladder control.** Does your child urinate a large amount at once, rather than dribbling a little at a time? Does he go several hours with a dry diaper, showing that he has the physical ability to hold his urine? Does he show you, by word or by standing in a particular way, that he needs to go?

• **Body control.** Can he walk confidently by himself? Can he pick up small objects, showing that he has the hand coordination needed to lower and raise a pair of loose-fitting pants?

• **Ability to follow directions.** Can your child point to several body parts on demand (nose, eyes, mouth, ears, etc.)? Will he follow requests to sit down and stand up? Can he bring you something from another room if you ask for it? Can he follow a two-part instruction, such as "Put the doll in the wagon" or "Get the book and give it to Daddy"?

One of the keys to success is preparing ahead of time. You need to make arrangements so that you can give your child your full attention, without any interruptions. You prepare several different tasty rewards, including lots of good things to drink. You also make a list of people whom your child cares about. This list might include, for example, Daddy, Grandma, and Uncle Fred, as well as make-believe characters such as Mickey or Barney. When you praise and encourage your child during the teaching session, you tell him how proud he is making each of these important people. This is a very powerful motivator. Before the actual teaching day, it's helpful to let your child become familiar with the potty, watch you in the bathroom, and learn the words to describe what's going on ("pee," "poop," "pants down," "wet," "dry," etc.).

The teaching itself makes use of several different techniques. These include practice with a doll, effective verbal instructions, guidance by hand, repetition, praise, rewards for dryness, and mildly unpleasant consequences (having to rush over to the potty and practice peeing several times) for being wet. Throughout the process, you give a lot of approval and tasty food and drink rewards, and you never punish or scold. You only show disapproval if your child wets, but it is done in a way that does not cause shame. As a result, many children find the process interesting and fun.

Advantages and disadvantages

I'm impressed that this method combines many effective teaching and motivation techniques in a powerful and positive way. It's easy to believe that a toddler who is developmentally ready could learn independent toileting in one day, although I have no personal experience with this approach. The authors have published a study to back up their claims. Out of 34 children, all but two of them were using the potty independently after training that lasted between 30 minutes and two days. A week later, they were all out of diapers, and were 99 percent accident free. Although the training focuses on peeing, most children learn to take charge of their pooping at the same time.

It's important to realize that this approach does not promise early toilet training. Most children will still need to be around two years of age when they start. But training may be complete several months sooner than when using the child-centered approach.

A possible disadvantage to this method is that you need to buy Azrin and Foxx's book and pay very close attention to the specific details of the training. Reading the book two or three times before starting is probably a good idea (it's a quick 192 pages). In published studies of parents using the book to train their children, results have been mixed. Some parents reported, for example, that their babies became very upset when they were criticized for having wet pants or made to practice walking over to the potty many times. When parents used the book with guidance from a child psychologist, however, results have been more uniformly positive.

So the book is not magic. But as long as you stay positive—no scolding, forcing, or punishment—I don't think you can do your child any harm. If she doesn't pick up on the toilet training as quickly as you think she should, or as quickly as the book promises, don't be discouraged. Just because highly skilled, experienced researchers got good results using this method, there's no guarantee that parents without special training— even really good parents—will be as successful. If you're willing to give your child and yourself a break for a couple of months, you can try again later. Another option is to consult with a behavioral specialist, who can coach you through the training process.

Practical tips
• **A potty seat is helpful when a child is just learning.** Most toddlers have a hard time balancing on an adult toilet seat, with their feet dangling in the air. And the feeling of insecurity makes it harder for them to relax and let go.

• **Bring along the potty.** When you're on the road with your toddler, you can throw a potty in the trunk of your car for easy access.

• **Remove the urine guard.** If your potty comes with a urine guard, think about taking it off. It's too easy for a little boy to scrape his penis on it, and turn sour about toilet training altogether.

• **Choose user-friendly clothing.** When you make the change to underwear, select clothing that's easy for your child to pull down and get back up on his own. That way, he'll be more independent.

• **Reinforce the training with stories.** There are many good picture books to help toddlers get the hang of the potty. Among my personal favorites: *Everyone Poops* by Taro Gomi and *Once Upon a Potty* by Alona Frankel.

SOME THINGS TO THINK ABOUT

Whichever approach you take to training, here are a few things to keep in mind:

• **Your mother or another helpful relative may have strong feelings about the right way to toilet train.** For example, you might think that you're being appropriately relaxed, but in this person's view, you're overly lax. The best way to deal with these opinions is to listen politely and then go ahead and do what feels right for you. You're the parent, after all, and even old family traditions may not be effective or fitting for your child.

• **Many parents worry that toilet training too early will cause psychological problems.** There isn't any good evidence that happens. However, toilet training that is rigid or harsh probably does have negative psychological effects.

• **Learning how to use the potty is only part of the training.** Learning how to wipe (front to back for girls, to prevent vaginal infections) and how to wash one's hands are also important.

• **For reasons no one understands, girls, in general, master toileting a few months before boys do.** If all of your friends have girls and you have a boy, don't be surprised if you're still changing diapers while they're picking out cool underpants.

• **Anytime a child makes developmental progress, there are bound to be episodes of backsliding.** Toilet training is no different. You can expect accidents after your toddler is first trained, and again when she is under stress.

• **Believe it or not, as a parent, you might have mixed feelings about the end of the diaper era.** Of course, it's great not to have to change diapers. But many parents also feel a tinge of loss when their babies move on in life. You can make up for the loss of togetherness during diaper changes by taking more time to play together, look at picture books, go for walks, and generally enjoy your child in ways you couldn't when you were both so wrapped up in diapers.

AFTERWORD

I've tried to make *Baby Basics* a very practical book, packed with useful advice on day-to-day topics like sleeping, eating, and diapering. But I'd like to conclude with another topic that, in its own way, is just as basic to raising a child: values.

When I ask parents what kind of adults they want their babies to become, the first answer I get is usually a general one: "I want my baby to be happy, to grow into a good person." Then I ask, "What do you mean, 'a good person'?" That's when parents tell me what is most important to them, their *values*. And, indeed, as a parent, your values are sure to color every part of your child's life, long before any formal religious or moral education takes effect. Your values come through in the way you hold your baby, talk to him, feed him, put him down to sleep, and even diaper him.

Different parents hold different ideals for what a good person should be. For some, what's most important is that their child grows up smart and successful. For others, respect for parents is the highest good. Your vision might be a child who grows up to fight for what's right, follow the law, care about other people, raise a big family, believe in God, make the world better, or something else entirely. Of course, your ideal can include several qualities, and it probably does. But only one or two can be at the top of your list. What are they?

Whatever your parenting values are, it's likely that many of the things you struggle with daily *don't* show up on your list. No parent tells me, "I want my son to grow up to sleep through the night" or "I want my daughter to become someone who is toilet trained." Taking the long view helps to put some of the immediate strains of child-rearing into perspective.

It's also very important to keep focused on the positive outcomes you want, rather than the negative ones you fear. Staying positive is hard to do nowadays. Newspapers and television shows surround us with stories about children gone bad. When your three-year-old smashes his toys in rage, it's natural to mentally flash to the teenager who shot up his school last week. You may need to remind yourself that your child is not that horribly disturbed youngster—he's just a frustrated toddler who hasn't yet learned good ways to handle his anger.

Your focus, positive or negative, comes out powerfully in the words you speak. When you tell your child, "I want you to be nice," your child thinks, "Mommy says I can be nice." When you say, "Stop being bad," your child thinks, "Mommy says I'm bad." The image you carry of your child and convey in your words helps shape the grown-up your child will become.

Of course, you do not have complete control over your child's future, or even his present. There are many aspects of your child—temperament, talents, and physical traits—that simply are what they are. You also can't control how other adults and children treat your child, especially as he gets older. But in the key area of values, what you do as a parent matters a great deal. Children learn values from their parents in two ways, through empathy and through limits.

Empathy
Underlying the golden rule—to treat others as you want to be treated yourself—is the concept of empathy. Empathy is the ability to put yourself in another person's place, to see things through her eyes and to feel what she feels. Babies as young as seven to nine months show empathy—becoming upset or worried if someone near them is crying, for example. By 18 months, many toddlers try to comfort their parents (and even sometimes their siblings) by bringing over a favorite teddy bear or blanket if they sense that their parents are sad or anxious. By three years of age, most children can accurately identify pictures of other children who are feeling sad, happy, or fearful.

Empathy is a natural instinct. It doesn't have to be taught. But when you show your child that you understand and care about how she feels, you strengthen her empathetic powers. When you treat your child with kindness and respect, she learns to approach the world in the same way. As your child grows, her ideas about right and wrong are sure to become more complicated and mature. But the empathy that you nurtured when she was still in diapers remains the foundation for her values.

Limits and discipline

Children have an instinct to care about others' feelings. They work hard for praise, and are often willing to give up a lot (e.g., pacifiers, diapers) to win their parents' approval. At the same time, children (like all of us) want what they want, when they want it. That's where limits come in.

Limits teach children that actions have consequences and that they can't always have what they desire. Learning about limits starts very early. A nursing baby who bites too hard on his mother's nipple learns that the feeding stops suddenly. A toddler who loves bedtime stories learns that story time eventually comes to an end each evening. Limit-setting has come up in every chapter of this book—around such topics as bedtime, meals, tantrums, etc.—because limits are simply part of life.

I can't leave the topic of limits without saying a few words about discipline and spanking. Many parents confuse discipline and punishment. Discipline means teaching a child what to do and what *not* to do. Effective discipline involves a lot of praise, encouragement, and positive role-modeling, along with a small amount of punishment. For children who are used to their parents' approval, perhaps the most effective punishment is simply to show disapproval. "I don't like it when you draw on the walls," said in a stern voice, does more to deter your future muralist than a swat on the behind. Parents who rely on punishment as their main form of discipline tend to have children who misbehave frequently, especially if they think they won't be caught.

Spanking and other physical punishments are never appropriate for little babies; they simply cannot comprehend why their beloved parents are hurting them. Most parents understand this and would never hit a baby. But many do believe in spanking for toddlers and older children. Among pediatricians and other professionals, there has been a great deal of debate, as well as some serious research, on the spanking question. As far as I can tell, the bottom line (so to speak) is that spanking itself is not the key issue—it's the quality of the spanking.

Children who are spanked arbitrarily and cruelly are more likely to grow up angry, afraid, and insensitive to others' distress. Spanking a child with a paddle or other object, or hitting a child anywhere other than the bottom, is potentially dangerous (and possibly illegal). On the other hand, children who are spanked with love and reason—yes, it *is* possible—often do just fine. For example, if your three-year-old has just run into the street and you want to impress upon him that he must never, *ever* do that again, you might choose to emphasize your words with a spanking. I'm not saying that you should respond in this way, only that no harm will come of it if you do.

Many parents raise terrific children without ever spanking. Others spank occasionally and still raise terrific children. But when parents tell me that they have to spank their children "all the time," it makes me think that they need to find other means of teaching right and wrong. Consistent, firm, and realistic limits are crucial; spanking is optional.

Trust yourself . . . and have fun

Dr. Benjamin Spock began his famous baby book with the words, "Trust yourself, you know more than you think you do." He wasn't only referring here to feeding, bathing, or diapers; he was talking about values. If you are like most parents, you already know how to nurture your child's natural empathy and how to provide sensible limits. Your instincts and common sense are reliable guides. Parenting instincts have their roots in our earliest memories. We remember what it felt like, as babies, to be loved and cared for. We can't put these memories into words, and we don't have to. We naturally give our babies the kind of loving care that nourished us.

It's different for parents who have had traumatic early childhood experiences—victims of child abuse, for example. They can't rely on their early memories to guide their parenting. One mother I knew, who had been abandoned as a toddler, couldn't bear to hear her baby crying. So she turned away, and her baby went hungry. Another parent, who had been severely abused, routinely slapped her two-year-old across the face and felt that this was the right thing to do.

I mention these sad cases because, remarkably, many people who were victims during their own childhoods still manage to be excellent parents. In order to avoid repeating the abuse, they watch themselves closely and make conscious decisions to treat their babies with kindness and consistency. They do not trust their parenting instincts completely. But they *do* trust in the power of their love to transform themselves into the kind of parents they never had.

So, in the end, I think "Trust yourself" is still the fundamental watchword. But I'd like to add another of my own: Have fun! Babies come with a built-in gauge that lets their parents know when they are healthy, secure, and learning: their smiles. Some express themselves with loud laughter, others with quiet concentration, but either way, the joy shows in their eyes. When you see that sparkle, you know that you're on the right path. Even more, look for those times when your child's joyful engagement is mirrored in your own delight—when you are having fun *together*. At these moments, you are building up a rich store of positive memories that can carry you both through the tough times that are also a part of growing up—through separation, fear, boredom, frustration, and conflict. And you are teaching your child one of the most important lessons anybody can learn: that life is about sharing happiness and other feelings with the people you love.

I hope this book is useful to you as you go about taking care of your baby—feeding her, changing her, comforting her, and putting her to sleep. Mostly, though, I hope that it helps you to trust yourself and *have fun* with your young child.

INDEX

INDEX

LaVergne, TN USA
03 November 2010

203411LV00001B/15/P